BERTRAND DE JOUVENEL

LIBRARY OF MODERN THINKERS

PUBLISHER: T. KENNETH CRIBB JR.

SERIES EDITOR: JEFFREY O. NELSON

PUBLISHED TITLES

ROBERT NISBET *by Brad Lowell Stone*

LUDWIG VON MISES *by Israel M. Kirzner*

WILHELM RÖPKE *by John Zmirak*

ERIC VOEGELIN *by Michael P. Federici*

BERTRAND DE JOUVENEL *by Daniel J. Mahoney*

FORTHCOMING

CHRISTOPHER DAWSON *by Gerald Russello*

WILL HERBERG *by Vigen Guroian*

WILLMOORE KENDALL *by George Carey*

CHRISTOPHER LASCH *by Alan Woolfolk*

ANDREW NELSON LYTLE *by Mark Malvasi*

JOHN COURTNEY MURRAY *by Marc Guerra*

MICHAEL OAKESHOTT *by Timothy Fuller*

MICHAEL POLANYI *by Mark Mitchell*

RICHARD WEAVER *by Steven Ealy*

FRANCIS GRAHAM WILSON *by H. Lee Cheek*

BERTRAND DE JOUVENEL

THE CONSERVATIVE LIBERAL AND THE ILLUSIONS OF MODERNITY

Daniel J. Mahoney

ASSUMPTION COLLEGE

ISI BOOKS

WILMINGTON, DELAWARE

The Library of Modern Thinkers is published in cooperation with Collegiate Network, Inc. Generous grants from the Sarah Scaife Foundation, Earhart Foundation, F. M. Kirby Foundation, Castle Rock Foundation, Pierre F. and Enid Goodrich Foundation, Wilbur Foundation, and the William H. Donner Foundation made this series possible. The Intercollegiate Studies Institute and Collegiate Network, Inc., gratefully acknowledge their support.

Mahoney, Daniel J., 1960–

    Bertrand de Jouvenel : the conservative liberal and the illusions of modernity / Daniel J. Mahoney. — 1st ed. — Wilmington, Del. : ISI Books, 2005.

        p. ; cm.
        (Library of modern thinkers)
        ISBN: 1932236406 (cloth)
        ISBN: 1932236414 (paper)

        1. Jouvenel, Bertrand de, 1903– 2. Political scientists—France—Biography. 3. Liberalism. 4. Political science. I. Title.

JC261 .M34 2005   2004104553
320/.092—dc22   0503

Published in the United States by:

    ISI Books
    In cooperation with Collegiate Network, Inc.
    Post Office Box 4431
    Wilmington, DE 19807-0431

Cover and interior design by Sam Torode
Manufactured in the United States of America

CONTENTS

PREFACE

BERTRAND DE JOUVENEL (1903–87) is one of a small number of twentieth-century political thinkers who truly matter, who are worthy of our continuing respect and attention. Yet his name is largely unknown in fashionable intellectual circles today, and his work has not come close to receiving the recognition it so richly merits. This book is above all an act of intellectual recovery, an effort to rectify the unwarranted neglect of one of the most thoughtful and humane political thinkers of the previous century.

A study of Jouvenel's thought necessarily entails a confrontation with the moral and political substance of the twentieth century since that "political milieu"—so "rife with political occurrences"—presented Jouvenel with much of the material on which he reflected.[1] From the beginning, Jouvenel was not content merely to make sense of his own situation or to anticipate the "possible futures" that lay before our democratic societies. He freely spoke of the "common good," "social friendship," and the "amenities of life," even as he attempted to come to terms with the political and intellectual pathologies that did so much to mar the last century of the second millennium. He defended the considerable achievements of the modern liberal democratic order but was dissatisfied with the anemic account of human nature and human motives that characterized the most influential currents of modern thought.

Jouvenel appealed to an older tradition of European reflection that affirmed the social nature of man and recognized the numerous reasons human beings have to be grateful for their civilized patrimony. The French political philosopher and social scientist was a conservative liberal who steered a principled middle path between reactionary nostalgia and progressive illusions, a student of man and society who never lost sight either of the truths that endure or of the essentially "dynamic" character of modern civilization. Jouvenel envisioned the diverse ways in which the permanent goods and truths of our nature could be sustained within an ever-changing and mobile social order. Against reactionaries and progressives alike, he resisted the temptation to put an end to things. There was no more penetrating critic of "the myth of the solution,"[2] of the pernicious illusion that the political problem could be permanently solved rather than prudently navigated or adjudicated. Jouvenel's unique blend of erudition, sobriety, urbanity, and civility has much to teach a "postmodern" age that has largely forgotten the moral and intellectual foundations of restraint, moderation, and intelligent deference to the wisdom of the past. He remains our contemporary in no small part because he was never unduly concerned with being relevant or up-to-date in his intellectual stances.

This book is on one level a continuation of my engagement with the French twentieth century (I have previously authored studies of Raymond Aron and Charles de Gaulle). It is also a continuation of my work on a series of thinkers (e.g., Aurel Kolnai, Pierre Manent, and Aleksandr Solzhenitsyn) who attempted to come to terms with both modern liberty and modern tyranny while doing justice to those "moral contents of life" that late modernity has so much difficulty affirming and sustaining. For his part, Jouvenel was a penetrating critic of twentieth-century tyranny and a qualified but genuine friend of the regime of modern liberty. His judgment was ultimately less steady and reliable than Aron's, but in some ways he surpassed his friend in philosophical depth and penetration. It is my deeply held conviction that these two great defenders of European liberty will be read long after Sartre, Althusser, Bourdieu, and Foucault have been relegated to the realm of ideological criticism, the fate of thinkers who will remain of interest primarily because their thought is so bereft of moral bearings or of an elementary sense of political responsibility. What Jouvenel once wrote about Aristotle, St. Thomas, and Montesquieu can be said with equal justice about both him and Aron: "in them is substance, and nothing of them is divorced from reality."[3]

Aristotle's god may be "thought thinking itself" but we mortals are, happily, sustained by community, conversation, and the generosity of friends and family. I have learned from Jouvenel the numerous ways in which every reflective human being must take himself for debtor. My family, particularly my mother and my now-departed father, has always provided unflagging support, love, and encouragement. Paul Seaton read every word in this book and provided invaluable suggestions, both editorial and substantive, along the way. My former student David DesRosiers, now vice president of the Manhattan Institute, wrote his dissertation on Jouvenel and has never lost his enthusiasm for someone he rightly regards as an intellectual treasure. David's enthusiasm for all things Jouvenelian has been truly infectious. Philippe Bénéton, Pierre Manent, Irving Louis Horowitz, and Peter Lawler have provided continuous friendship, sage advice, and much encouragement for me to bring Jouvenel's achievement to the attention of a broader public audience. Brian Anderson, Stephen Gardner, Ralph Hancock, Marc Guerra, and Nalin Ranasinghe have been trusted interlocutors on every aspect of political and intellectual life. I am grateful to them and other friends, including the members of our small fraternity of Solzhenitsyn aficionados, who help make the intellectual life a joy rather than a chore or a mere profession. I would also like to thank Janet Truscott and Carmella Murphy, who provided invaluable help with computer-related issues and greatly facilitated the appearance of the manuscript. No expression of my debts would be complete without mentioning the Earhart Foundation of Ann Arbor, Michigan. Under the leadership first of David Kennedy and now of Ingrid Gregg, Earhart has provided generous support for my various scholarly endeavors. Timely grants from that foundation have given me the leisure to complete this book as well as my earlier works on Aron, de Gaulle, and Solzhenitsyn. The Earhart Foundation has consistently shown itself to be a friend of liberal learning and of conservative liberal thought in its various forms.

A final word of thanks is owed to my editor Jeremy Beer. It is a delight to have an editor who not only is deeply conversant with ideas but who promotes their clear and efficacious expression. I am happy to count Jeremy among my friends.

A version of chapter 3 appeared in the *Political Science Reviewer* (volume 32, 2003, 93–117) and in French translation as "Liberté et bien commun chez Bertrand de Jouvenel" in *Commentaire* (number 103, Autumn 2003, 623–35). In chapter 1, I have freely drawn on several paragraphs of my introduction (written in conjunction with David M. DesRosiers) to the 1997 Liberty Fund edition of *Sovereignty: An Inquiry into the Political Good.* I am grateful to all concerned for permission to reprint these materials.

Daniel J. Mahoney
Worcester, Massachusetts
October 29, 2004

ABBREVIATIONS

ER   *The Ethics of Redistribution* (Indianapolis, IN: Liberty Fund, 1990). Originally published by Cambridge University Press in 1952.

OP   *On Power: The Natural History of Its Growth* (Indianapolis, IN: Liberty Fund, 1993). Translated by J. F. Huntington. English-language edition originally published by Viking Press in 1948.

PT   *The Pure Theory of Politics* (Indianapolis, IN: Liberty Fund, 2000). Originally published in the United States by Yale University Press in 1963.

S   *Sovereignty: An Inquiry into the Political Good* (Indianapolis, IN: Liberty Fund, 1997). Translated by J. F. Huntington. English-language edition originally published in the United States by the University of Chicago Press in 1957.

CHAPTER ONE

INTRODUCTION: THE ITINERARY OF A CONSERVATIVE LIBERAL

Great necessities, angers, and enthusiasms have made us impatient toward everything that stops the will and slows action. . . .

[But] wills must acknowledge limits. We have dearly learned old truths that periodically are erased from the social memory: rights exist that it is not just to offend, rules that it isn't prudent to violate. Respect for these rights and these rules imposes itself even when transgressing them appears to provide an opportunity to remedy a great evil or procure a great good. For there is no more profound or durable evil than their discredit, there is no more salutary and fecund good than their being placed outside of assault and attack.[1]

— Bertrand de Jouvenel

WHY A BOOK ON THE French political thinker Bertrand de Jouvenel, the overwhelmed contemporary reader may be tempted to ask. He was, after all, in the judgment of Dennis Hale and Marc Landy, "the least famous of the great political thinkers of the twentieth century."[2] But his relative lack of fame in no way qualifies the genuine greatness of his thought. There are many reasons to recommend the rediscovery of this unduly neglected thinker. To begin with, Jouvenel's voluminous oeuvre managed to combine profound theoretical reflection with remarkable attentiveness to the issues of the age. His work scrupulously addressed the present age without ever losing sight of those permanent verities that inform responsible thought and action. Furthermore, as Pierre Manent has pointed out, Jouvenel had the additional merit of writing with eloquence and charm in an era that too often succumbed to the spirit of abstraction and the allure of "scientificity."[3] He was a civic-minded moralist as much as a political philosopher and social scientist. In the spirit of his two great nineteenth-century inspirations, Benjamin Constant and Alexis de Tocqueville, he renewed an older wisdom that recognized that "there are things too heavy for human hands."[4] Like these forebears, he set out to rescue liberalism from that revolutionary inebriation that refused to bow before any sacred limits or restraints. Jouvenel never succumbed to the temptation of confusing the Good with an unfolding historical process or with the unfettered will of the one, the few, or the many, even as he accepted the inevitability and desirability of the open or dynamic society. He was the conservative liberal par excellence, a principled critic of progressive illusions who fully appreciated the folly of attempting to stand athwart the historical adventure that is modernity.

In the years before World War II Bertrand de Jouvenel made a living from journalism.[5] He wrote for such prominent newspapers as *Le Petit Journal* and *Paris Soir*. During those years he became a practitioner of political celebrity journalism and had occasion to interview a host of famous statesmen—and tyrants—such as David Lloyd George, Neville Chamberlain, Winston Churchill, Mussolini, and Hitler (as we shall see, his controversial interview with Hitler would haunt him for the rest of his life, even though it was considered to be something of a coup at the time of its publication). In the years after 1945 he was simultaneously a journalist, professor (he taught or lectured at various times at Oxford, Cambridge, Cal-Berkeley, Yale, and at the Institut d'études politiques and the Faculty of Law and Economic Sciences of the University of Paris), political philosopher, political commentator, and pioneer author of sober, economically literate, and philosophically informed excursions into ecology and "future studies." He thus brought to his writings the powers of description typical of a journalist, the philosopher's appreciation of enduring and universal truths, and an admirable openness to the contribution that social science could make toward understanding the transformations characteristic of modern life. In addition, his writings go a long way toward recovering the classical understanding of political science as the architectonic science whose ultimate subject matter is nothing less than the comprehensive good for human beings.[6] In important respects, then, Jouvenel's work bridges classicism and modernism, political philosophy and social science, the traditionalist's preoccupation with "the good life" and the enlightenment Left's preference for the open or dynamic society.

Bertrand de Jouvenel was a Frenchman intimately familiar with and sympathetic toward the United States; his English (spoken with an American accent) was impeccable. He regularly acknowledged the indispensable contribution that Britain, the cradle of parliamentary liberty, had made to the cause of freedom in the modern world, and he wrote respectfully, even admiringly, about the American constitutional order (the gravitas that still marked the United States Senate in the 1950s particularly impressed him).[7] It is not surprising, therefore, that he was the first French political thinker of any note to rediscover the political wisdom of what might be called the "English school" of French political philosophers, those nineteenth-century French liberals such as Constant, Guizot, and Tocqueville who were horrified by revolutionary despotism and who admired the civility and moderation characteristic of Anglo-American political life. Yet for reasons that will be fully explored in the final chapter of this work, Jouvenel has yet to receive his rightful measure of recognition in his native land. In France his reputation has been marred by the lingering impression that he was a collaborator of sorts during the Second World War (he was not) and by the fact that he committed two major faux pas in the period leading up to the war,[8] the first being his aforementioned interview with Adolph Hitler in February 1936 (we will explore this issue at greater length in chapter 7 of this book), and the second his ill-advised membership in Jacques Doriot's Parti populair français (PPF) from 1936 until 1938.

Thus, though there is no shortage of self-proclaimed "liberal" political thinkers in France today, few explicitly acknowledge indebtedness to the political philosophizing of Bertrand de Jouvenel (the intellectual circles around the journals *Commentaire* and *Futuribles* are something of an exception in this regard). In France he remains a rather marginal figure best remembered for his 1945 classic *On Power* and for his forays into political ecology and future studies. Indeed, Jouvenel's intellectual achievement has never been fully acknowledged by either the French general public or intellectual establishment, not even by those who share his core philosophical principles. As a result, some of Jouvenel's most important theoretical works are not even in print in France today (this is the case with both *Sovereignty* and *The Pure Theory of Politics*), while many more of his major works are available once again in the United States (thanks especially to the good offices of Liberty Fund and Transaction Publishers). In the English-speaking world, in fact, Jouvenel is now considered to be a political philosopher of some importance, one of the most penetrating conservative-minded thinkers of the twentieth century.

In the years between 1945 and 1968, Jouvenel produced an impressive body of work belonging to the tradition known as conservative liberalism. These writings explored the inexorable growth of state power in modern times, the difficult but necessary task of articulating a conception of the common good appropriate to a dynamic, "progressive" society, and the challenge of formulating a political science that could reconcile tradition and change while preserving the freedom and dignity of the individual.

Jouvenel was far from doctrinaire in his approach to political matters. A critic of the centralizing propensities of the state, he nonetheless appreciated that political authority was indispensable for maintaining social trust as well as economic equilibrium. A charter member of the classical liberal Mont Pélerin Society (whose leading light was the distinguished economist and social theorist F. A. Hayek), he rejected the individualist premises underlying modern economics and reminded his contemporaries that the good life entailed something more fundamental than the maximization of individual preferences.[9] In his mature writings, Jouvenel vigorously challenged the "progressivist" conceit at the heart of modern thought, the illusion that social and economic development necessarily entail moral progress. But he never rejected modernity per se. The coherence and insight that characterize Jouvenel's synthesis is perhaps the foremost reason for studying him today.

Beyond Facile Progressivism: How Jouvenel Became Jouvenel

In decisive respects, Jouvenel was a child of his time. But he can properly be called a political philosopher precisely because he ultimately succeeded in transcending the progressivism that was the dominant prejudice of his age. This was no easy feat. Jouvenel was born in 1903 into a milieu that more or less took the inevitability of progress for granted. His father, Henri de Jouvenel, was an influential politician and respected journalist, a sometime Dreyfusard, a member of the Senate of the Third French Republic, and the French representative to the League of Nations in Geneva.[10] He was, as Pierre Hassner has put it, "a constant fighter for liberal causes."[11] His mother, Sarah Boas, came from a thoroughly assimilated Jewish family. She was a cultivated, caring woman who ran a famous Parisian salon and played a not insignificant role in the creation of the modern Czechoslovakian state.[12] Jouvenel's stepmother was the redoubtable novelist Colette, with whom he even had a youthful affair.[13] "The entire Jouvenel family," writes Hassner, "was aristocratic, political, and literary."[14] Jouvenel's urbane parents embodied the best of the antebellum spirit, of a civilized progressivism that seemed to be the inevitable future of a Europe that had finally mastered its social passions. But the Great War would change everything. As Jouvenel wrote with hindsight, in those years Europe had "marched toward an apocalypse" as if "demons breathed their strength to ferocious agents and blinded the well-intentioned."[15] But it took Jouvenel three decades to fully liberate himself from facile progressivism, to genuinely appreciate that there was "no natural" and upward "course of history,"[16] that war and tyranny remain ever-present human possibilities.

Bertrand de Jouvenel wrote about the first forty-two years of his life with grace, eloquence, and no small note of pathos in his 1979 memoir *Un Voyageur dans le siècle*.[17] This work provides a fascinating account of Jouvenel's youthful intellectual and political itinerary and is indispensable for understanding the sinuous path by which he arrived at his mature intellectual orientation. Nor is it of merely biographical interest. Jouvenel's "spectator's narrative" quickly becomes "the lament of a generation"[18] (the one born between 1899 and 1907)[19] that had been too young to serve in the war, had repudiated bellicose passions, and had committed itself to noble ideals of social reform and Franco-German reconciliation. Jouvenel's generation, thoroughly decent but blinded by excessive hopes, was destined to recover a sense of historical tragedy only at the terrible price of experiencing the consequences of the decomposition of and assaults on the European bourgeois order. Jouvenel and his coevals experienced forms of war and tyranny that had been literally unthinkable to those who had been accustomed to take the achievements of liberal civilization for granted.

Jouvenel's reconsideration of painful events and memories was, he writes in the preface to his memoir, nothing less than a "sort of descent into Hell."[20] Throughout the 1960s and '70s, Jouvenel's professional life had been focused on exploring "possible futures" (in light of enduring political and philosophical questions, to be sure),[21] and neither introspection nor self-evaluation came naturally to him.[22] He freely admits that he was less than eager to confront his own "faux pas" or to relive the terrible drama by which Europe was "carried away by the Furies and [lost] its civilized countenance."[23] Nonetheless, he mustered the courage to do so with impressive penetration and honesty.

Most of Jouvenel's American readers know little about Jouvenel's intellectual itinerary and are not usually aware that he was not always the sober conservative liberal political thinker of his major writings of the postwar period. The young Jouvenel dreamed of a "new order"—not the militarized state and society trumpeted by totalitarians of the Left and Right, but a pacified, cosmopolitan liberal order where an energetic state would limit the "anarchy" of the market without in any way threatening fundamental human liberties. Still, because of his deep-seated commitment to liberal freedoms, Jouvenel from the beginning rejected a command-and-control approach to the management and regulation of the economic order. Even as a moderately leftist critic of the established social order, he affirmed the broad principles of what would later come to be called a "social market" economy. He later regretted calling his first book *L'économie dirigée* (The Directed Economy), since it created the impression that he supported efforts to substitute the heavy-handedness of the state for the free initiatives that naturally emanate from civil society.[24] Even in this youthful work, published in 1928, Jouvenel adamantly rejected the fashionable idea that "the hour of initiatives" was somehow a thing of the past.[25] He favored a modest version of "indicative planning": in his view, the state should limit itself to establishing conditions that are truly conducive to balanced economic and social development. But the individual as owner, producer, and consumer must remain free to act.[26] The state should neither own the "means of production" nor dictate the forms of particular economic enterprises. At the age of twenty-three, Jouvenel perceptively warned about the danger of a "shackled" economy that aimed to replace the market with the cumbersome intrusions of an allegedly omnicompetent state.[27] Even as a youthful socialist, Jouvenel appreciated that such pretensions would lead to social petrification or worse and did nothing to advance the prospects for a humane economy.

Nevertheless, Jouvenel maintained that a bold strategy of political and economic reform was required to overcome the European social crisis that was tearing apart the moral and physical fabric of the liberal order throughout the 1930s. He came to believe that laissez-faire economic policies had failed miserably and that the state must take a much more proactive role in addressing the "scandal" of unemployment and overcoming the social crisis of the age.[28] This preoccupation with the evils of mass unemployment and the failure of established economic models is particularly evident in his 1933 book *La crise du capitalisme américain*.[29] Jouvenel had no fundamental illusions about either Communist or Nazi totalitarianism, even if he didn't take the full measure of either until he composed *On Power* during his Swiss exile in 1943 and 1944. But he remained clearly focused on the crisis of the Western democratic world and welcomed efforts at bold experimentation to overcome unemployment and to set the social order aright again. He despised fascist tyranny but at the same time showed some indulgence for the mobilization of society that was a central feature of revolutionary despotism. In the 1930s, Jouvenel seemed to lose sight of the dangers that necessarily accompany the unleashing of state power even at the service of necessary reforms. In the face of a truly unprecedented social crisis, Jouvenel for a time succumbed to the impatience that is one of the hallmarks of the modern intellectual.

Bertrand de Jouvenel's mature political philosophy arose from his experience of modern tyranny and from reflection on his own intellectual and political misjudgments in the period leading up to World War II.[30] This experience and reflection convinced him of the indispensability of liberal constitutionalism and of the need to rethink its moral foundations. Earlier, in the prewar period, he had lost faith in the powers of renewal of the French Third Republic if not of liberal democracy itself. Looking for means to revitalize France, he had joined the Parti populaire français, a right-wing populist party headed by an ex-Communist by the name of Jacques Doriot.[31] He left the party in late 1938 in no small part because of the PPF's support of the Munich Pact and the political dismemberment of Czechoslovakia (Jouvenel had served as personal secretary to that country's foreign minister—later to be president—Edward Benes in the spring of 1924 and had long-standing personal and political ties to the Czechoslovakian democracy).[32]

While never fascist or protofascist in any sense of these terms (contrary to the ludicrous distortion put forward by the Israeli historian Zeev Sternhell in an indiscriminate assault on Jouvenel in his controversial book *Neither Right Nor Left*),[33] Jouvenel nonetheless was impressed by the relative vitality of the totalitarian regimes in contrast to the weakness and decadence of the European democracies. This strain of thought is most evident—and disturbing—in his 1941 tract *Après la défaite*,[34] published during the Occupation. In that work he contrasts the youthful renewal and communal tendencies of the totalitarian regimes with the corruption and decomposition of "liberal" Europe.

Despite his agonizing doubts about the prospects for Europe's liberal democracies, Jouvenel was neither a collaborator nor an apologist for Nazi totalitarianism. But as a secret intelligence officer for the Service de Renseignements de l'Armée française, Jouvenel was ordered to maintain contacts with his old friend Otto Abetz, at that time the German ambassador to occupied France (in the late 1920s the two had begun to develop a close friendship as a result of their common commitment to Franco-German reconciliation).[35] His mission was to clarify German intentions toward unoccupied France at a time (well before November 1942) when Vichy was still something less than a puppet of the Nazi regime. Such so-called fraternizing undoubtedly contributed to the widespread impression that Jouvenel had collaborated with the German authorities at least in the early years of the war. In fact, by 1942 Jouvenel had already joined the French Resistance in his native Corrèze. In *Un Voyageur dans le siècle* Jouvenel discusses his growing realization that the Vichy regime was becoming a servile instrument of the totalitarian Nazi state. He reports his genuine shock in hearing Pierre Laval, a man who had four times served as premier of the French Republic, state on the radio on June 22, 1942 (the first anniversary of the German invasion of Soviet Russia), that he "hoped for the victory of Germany" in the war.[36] After it became clear that the Germans suspected his resistance activities and that he was likely to be arrested, Jouvenel and his wife Hélène fled to freedom in neutral Switzerland. There he researched and completed *On Power* (published in French in Switzerland in early 1945 and in English in 1948).[37] It was that famous work that marked his turn to a realistic and anti-totalitarian liberalism.

Jouvenel's Trilogy

Jouvenel's major achievement as a political philosopher is a trilogy of political reflection published between 1945 and 1963, of which *On Power* is the first volume. But the character of the trilogy as a unified intellectual project is practically unknown in this country. His Tocquevillian analysis of the rise of the centralized state, the "Minotaur," as he famously calls it in *On Power*, is often cited. So too is his lucid critique of the disastrous moral and political consequences of redistributionism in *The Ethics of Redistribution* (originally published by Cambridge University Press in 1952).[38] But a narrow focus on these works has led some to pigeonhole Jouvenel as an anticollectivist or classical liberal thinker. In truth, Jouvenel was neither a conventional classical liberal nor a traditionalist, even if his thought owes something fundamental to both currents of thought. Jouvenel's other major works, particularly

Sovereignty: An Inquiry into the Political Good (1955)[39] and *The Pure Theory of Politics* (1963),[40] which together with *On Power* constitute his trilogy on politics, are far less familiar to both French and American readers. Yet these works are arguably his most important because they deal with first principles. In fact, *On Power* is a kind of prolegomenon both to the positive account of liberty and the common good provided in *Sovereignty* and to his later effort to revitalize and modernize classical political science in *The Pure Theory of Politics*.

On Power provides an illuminating account of the erosion of intermediate institutions and responsible individuality at the hands of twentieth-century totalitarian regimes as well as by the "social protectorates" established in contemporary democratic societies.[41] Responding to this situation, *The Pure Theory of Politics* outlines the possibility of a political science that is genuinely "behavioral" in character and explores new ways to maintain and renew constitutional government.[42] In this work Jouvenel demonstrates that those who are concerned with maintaining political liberty and civility must master the "game" of politics if they are to succeed. Whether analyzing the social framework of human freedom, the ways in which a few men such as Cassius inspire others to great or notorious deeds (such as the assassination of Caesar), or contemplating the disruptive effects of determined minorities on democratic societies, Jouvenel illustrates the elementary foundation of political action in the capacity of some human beings to move other human beings. He thereby provides the basis for a realistic political science sensitive to the Machiavellian machinations of those who seek to subvert civilized political communities. *Sovereignty,* the central and connecting work in the trilogy, delineates a dynamic conception of the political good that does justice to the requirements of modern liberty. As Pierre Hassner has rightly observed, *Sovereignty* "holds the key to the passage from the historical approach of [*On Power*] to the analytic perspective of [*The Pure Theory of Politics*]."[43] It is a major contribution to political philosophy that amply rewards repeated study and reflection.

It is in *Sovereignty* that Jouvenel attempts to liberate the indispensable notion of the common good from the "prison of the corollaries,"[44] that is, from its historical identification with the small, homogenous polis recommended by political philosophers such as Plato and Rousseau. Jouvenel reveals the covert complicity that connects the romantic reactionary and the subversive revolutionary: both parties want to "put an end to history" by creating (or recreating) a harmonious city free of conflict and above the messy contingencies of history. The remarkable equanimity of *Sovereignty* lies precisely in its principled refusal to succumb to either reactionary nostalgia or revolutionary impatience. The "common good" is not a once-and-for-all achievement but rather a never wholly accomplished effort at civic amity that guides the acting citizen and statesman within every existing social order. More deeply, Jouvenel rejects the modernist conceit that man is his own maker and can found a viable human order solely on the principle of the human will. Instead he recommends a spirit of moderation that will allow democratic statesmen and citizens to combine respect for innovation and individual freedom with the recognition that every human order must bow before the permanent verities that ground and guide human freedom and responsibility.

Because of their unforced union of theoretical penetration and
practical good sense, I have chosen to concentrate on the political
and philosophical reflection of the mature Jouvenel that is con-
tained in these three masterworks of political philosophy. But this
book is likewise informed by an attentive study of Jouvenel's early
and late writings, particularly his urbane and instructive essays
written between 1945 and 1976, his writings on political economy,
and his little-known but quite revealing and instructive 1983 book
on Marx and Engels (*Marx et Engels: La longue marche*).[45] This
variegated body of work is not without its underlying coherence. It
is the thesis of this book that Jouvenel was one of the few great
thinkers of the twentieth century to challenge the "fearful and atheistic individualism" undergirding philosophical modernity while
defending the undeniable achievements of modern constitutionalism.[46] Jouvenel's work bridges classical, Christian, and modern
thought in a way that does justice to the social nature of man, the
givenness of the world, and the freedom that is a precondition of
true human dignity and responsibility. Jouvenel was not alone in
undertaking such a project. His affinities with Leo Strauss and Eric
Voegelin (the two thinkers most responsible for the revival of classical political philosophy in our time) will be readily apparent to
many readers of this book. Like them, Jouvenel welcomes citizenship in the modern world without succumbing to the hubris that
is all too typical of modernist or progressivist thought. His mature
thought has the additional merit of resisting the illusions of modernity without advocating a simple return to either the theory or
the practice of the premodern world.

Beyond the "Civilization of Power": Affections, Manners, and Natural Piety

I have called Jouvenel a "conservative liberal" for reasons that ought to have become readily apparent. But in important respects his writings ultimately resist ideological classification. They combine searching textual exegesis of classic political and philosophical texts, the insights and warnings of a sturdy if genteel moralist, and discerning analysis of institutions and unfolding political, social, and economic realities. An article of his might typically bring together elegant reflections on the Roman tribunate or the French parlements, the writings of Tocqueville or Sismondi, and the moral foundations of law, with detailed attention to state-of-the-art social science research. At the same time, Jouvenel never lost sight of the fact that "affections" and "manners" were at the heart of political science rightly understood. It was for his abiding recognition of this fact that Rousseau remained Jouvenel's "favorite author."[47] In Jouvenel's considered judgment, a social science that aspires to understand human beings must never lose sight of the question of what deserves our love and what ought to inspire our admiration.[48] As Jouvenel told an interviewer in 1970, both Marxists and liberals pay far too little attention to the manners, morals, and affections that bind the civil order and give social life its texture, dignity, and grandeur.[49] Unfortunately, modern men were all too often in the thrall of the "civilization of power"[50] and so frequently succumbed to the delusion that the purpose of life is coextensive with the unending accumulation and provision of goods and services. They therefore were apt to neglect or dismiss the affections and sentiments, the manners and formalities, that lead self-absorbed men to "treat each other with consideration."[51] It is important to note, however, that Jouvenel never addressed these matters in an abstract or didactic manner; in *Revoir Hélène*, for example, he paid moving tribute to his beloved wife and best friend of over thirty years, Hélène Duseingneur de Jouvenel, who died of cancer in the mid-1970s.[52] It was in this manner that he provided his readers with a concrete illustration of the power of the affections to elevate the human heart. Jouvenel managed to pull off the rare feat of writing about manners, affections, and social friendship without a trace of sentimentality or political utopianism.

Jouvenel thought well, sometimes too well, of individual human beings (this good-natured tendency of taking individual human beings at their word probably led him to be unduly impressed by Hitler when he interviewed him in 1936 and by the good intentions of student radicals in May 1968). But he came to have no illusions whatsoever about the inevitability of political progress or about the growing rationality of the human race. He knew that things were always getting better and worse at the same time, to cite the felicitous formulation of Peter Augustine Lawler. As evidence of the lack of progress in political judgment Jouvenel told an interviewer in 1970 that while Nicias had warned the Athenian assembly about the imprudence of the Syracusan expedition and Adolphe Thiers had issued prescient warnings against French intervention in Mexico in 1864, no prominent American statesman had delivered a great discourse anticipating future difficulties in Vietnam. (And, he added, those who came to most "ardently denounce" the Vietnam War did nothing to "avert" it in the first place.)[53] Whatever his personal failings of political judgment, Jouvenel's mature works are informed by a profound sense of historical tragedy. In *The Pure Theory of Politics*, he offers the hard truth that the great political dislocations, historical tragedies, and human passions described so luminously in the narrative of Thucydides or the political dramas of Shakespeare are ever-present human possibilities.[54] The experiences of the French Revolution and of totalitarianism in the twentieth century in particular revealed the vulnerability of a politics of civility to disruption by illiberal, tyrannical forces. This is the theme of Jouvenel's elegant and searching conclusion to the final section of *Pure Theory*, "The Manners of Politics," and is explored at some length in chapter 6 of this book.[55]

Jouvenel was a Frenchman who took his Christian faith seriously even if he eschewed sectarian or ostentatious displays of piety. As we shall see, some of his works, particularly *On Power* and *Sovereignty*, are imbued with a deep if discreet Catholic sensibility. In this connection, he joined a series of conservative-minded political philosophers who exposed the malign political consequences of "the emancipation of the [human] will" and set about to recover a sense of those natural moral limits that frame human freedom and are a precondition of our real dignity as human beings.[56] Jouvenel's reader cannot help but be impressed by the rich evocation of natural, familial, and ecological piety that informs his work as a whole. Jouvenel's writings convey a profound appreciation of the "givenness" of things and articulate the myriad reasons why gratitude is the appropriate response of human beings to their situation in the world. As he told an interviewer from *L'Express* in

1972, he believed that "the sentiment of what one has, appreciating what is given to us, is an homage to God."[57] For Jouvenel, "sentiments of affection, of respect, and love," informed by a sense of gratitude for the gratuitousness of being, provide human beings with access to the divine whole.[58] "The wise man knows himself for debtor,"[59] writes Jouvenel in *Sovereignty*. Jouvenel thus had no sympathy for the intellectual conceits that dominated modern thought. Notions such as the "state of nature," the "autonomous self," or the "creative" individual who aspired to be "beyond good and evil" were all based on willful denials of the social nature of man and the manifold reasons to affirm the givenness and goodness of human life.

Jouvenel's sensitive appreciation of the integrity of the natural order of things informed his defense of "political ecology" in contrast to the Cartesian project of limitless human mastery over nonhuman nature.[60] To the modern project's evocation of the "mastery of nature for the relief of man's estate," Jouvenel preferred to think of the earth as man's "home," toward which he had a special obligation of stewardship. The image of "gardening" came naturally to his pen whenever he discussed economic and ecological matters. For example, he wrote in his diaries with heartfelt affection about the trees of his native Corrèze.[61] In Jouvenel's view, it was not mere sentimentality that led human beings to "venerate" trees. The tree was rooted in the land itself and provided a constant reminder of those things that do not pass away. Rousseau had written that "the breath of man is mortal to man." Jouvenel took this insight most seriously indeed. The "civilization of power" came at a great price, one that undermined natural piety and that risked the permanent poisoning and scarring of the natural environment. But science has also shown that the continual regeneration of forests provides invaluable protection against the poisoning of our earthly home. Jouvenel's poetic invocation of the dignity of trees is aimed less at nature worship than at renewing a sense of human responsibility for our natural home. Commonsense environmentalism, attuned to the insights of economic science, could rekindle a practical appreciation of the limits of what Jouvenel sometimes called the "ephemeral civilization."[62] Despite its undeniable achievements, modern industrial civilization depends on the "law of accelerated destruction."[63] The consumer goods of the modern economy are in no way made to last. Even our lodgings are deliberately made with obsolescence in mind. In contrast, to this utilitarian vision that privileges creative destruction over permanence, Jouvenel defended "the culture of the garret,"[64] a world where human beings maintained ties to the past and built (and kept) things that evoked gratitude, and were thus not motivated merely by the economic imperative of progress, with its accompanying creative innovation and destruction. Our lodgings and landscapes should help shape a spirit of piety rather than the self-defeating illusion that we are gods who make ourselves anew with each passing generation. In keeping with the dialectical equanimity of his thought, Jouvenel also understood the value of private property and the indispensability of individual initiative, the latter for the moral health and economic viability of modern societies. He had no illusions whatsoever about the ability of collectivism to produce a humane alternative to the civilization of power, to the ephemeral civilization.[65] He knew that the conquest of nature was inseparable from the blessings of modern liberty. But if its logic was carried through to the bitter end, the Promethean self-confidence of modern man risked destroying the very preconditions of our humanity.

Prudence and the "Art of Conjecture"

It was for this reason, among others, that in the final stages of his career Jouvenel turned to the study of "prevision." In the 1960s and '70s he directed SEDEIS (La Societé d'étude et de documentation économique, industrielle, et sociale) and was the guiding hand behind its journals *Chroniques S.E.D.E.I.S.* and *Analyse et prévision* (the "futurist" journal *Futuribles* arose out of these earlier ventures and is now ably edited by his son Hugues de Jouvenel). By this time, he had come to appreciate that the prudent man must reflect assiduously on the possible outcomes of the modern adventure and do his best to steer modern liberty toward "the perpetration of the good."[66] Jouvenel aimed to reconnect human initiative with its manifold moral dimensions, which requires the recovery of a full sense of man's obligation to the great "contract" that binds the living, the dead, and the as yet unborn. Jouvenel thus spent twenty years of his life reflecting on how the "amenities of life,"[67] the spiritual and material goods that are necessary for human happiness and flourishing, might be preserved within the ephemeral civilization. This was also, in his view, part of the task of social science. He believed that the social scientist has a special professional obligation to anticipate trouble, to analyze and to suggest how to ward off those social and political forces that might promote tyranny and fanaticism or undermine civility and social comity. In an important essay, "Political Science and Prevision," originally published in the *American Political Science Review* in 1965,[68] Jouvenel spoke of the political scientist's obligation to help cultivate foresight in public men even as he cautioned about the necessarily "probabilistic" character of conjecture.[69] For him, the cultivation of prudence or foresight was a moral obligation for all agents; it would remain sterile, however, if it remained at the level of mere "precept."[70] Foresight must be transformed from a noble precept to a practical skill if prudence is to find its rightful place in the human city. Jouvenel's professional preoccupation with "possible futures" thus was the furthest thing from naïve idealism or reckless political utopianism. Jouvenel hoped to give a more "systematic" form to the virtue of prudence, he wished to discipline futurist speculation, to articulate a "utopianism divorced from illusion" that was tied to social science research and informed by philosophical reflection.[71]

His 1964 book *The Art of Conjecture* (published in English in 1967) provides the imitable model of such a humane, disciplined, and morally serious futurism.[72] In this impressive work, Jouvenel insists that the future cannot be known with any kind of certainty. At best, "possible futures" ("futuribles") can be limned. Jouvenel's self-described task is a modest but demanding one: to make the discussion of the "possible" a "trifle more rigorous."[73]

Jouvenel freely accepts Raymond Aron's and Karl Popper's critiques of "facile optimism" and "historicist" thinking.[74] He also provides an excellent critique of "system-based modes of prediction" of the kind famously developed by Comte and Marx.[75] His chapter on Thucydides and game theory shows how the art of conjecture is inherent in the very nature of decision-making and therefore is essential to the cultivation of prudential judgment. Game theory, in contrast, presupposes a "limited, predetermined set of possible futures."[76] It narrows or truncates what is possible. Game theory is not so rigorous or scientific after all.

Jouvenel ably shows how "prevision" becomes ever more important in the dynamic society, in a world where custom and precedent can no longer be relied on to predict or guide human behaviors.[77] But Jouvenel's goal remains broadly conservative and admirably humanistic: he aims to prevent human beings from becoming the playthings of history and technology, mere objects of inexorable forces, and thus to avoid C. S. Lewis's "abolition of man."[78] To illustrate the dangers inherent in a certain kind of futurist speculation, Jouvenel even provides an instructive and entertaining account of famous, misguided predictions in the past.[79] *The Art of Conjecture* not only limns a morally serious, antiscientistic futurism that links good sense to social science; it also provides his readers with a splendid classical liberal education along the way. Jouvenel's futurist writings are thus less a departure from his intellectual itinerary than they are a concrete illustration of the ability of this essentially conservative man to fully engage the problems and issues of the contemporary world.

Conclusion

Bertrand de Jouvenel's practical judgments were not always beyond reproach. He was a less sure-footed guide to history-in-the making than was his close friend and contemporary Raymond Aron (although Jouvenel was in some respects a deeper, more philosophical thinker). Aron was right about all the key issues of the age (especially those related to the protracted conflict between liberal democracy and totalitarianism that dominated the greater part of the twentieth century) and was more successful than Jouvenel in illustrating the enduring relevance of Tocquevillian wisdom for grappling with the dilemmas of modern society.[80] In the seventh and final chapter of this book we will explore the tension between Jouvenel's considerable theoretical achievement and the occasional unsteadiness and unreliability of his practical judgment. But Aron was certainly right, when responding to the calumnies of Zeev Sternhell, to observe that Jouvenel was not only "one of the two or three leading political thinkers of his generation" but a man who was "worthy of respect, even with regard to [his] mistakes."[81] This book hopes to demonstrate that the enduring wisdom of Jouvenel's great postwar writings far outweighs the misjudgments, real or imagined, that have so far inhibited him from attaining the full recognition he merits in his native France.

CHAPTER TWO

TAMING THE MINOTAUR:
THE NATURE AND
LIMITS OF POWER

BERTRAND DE JOUVENEL WAS (in the self-description of Alexis de
Tocqueville) "a strange kind of liberal." He loved liberty and believed
in the moral equality of men but resisted every form of egalitarian
dogmatism. He was deeply critical of the various abstractions that did
so much to distort modern political reflection. He was convinced
that the "state of nature" was a fiction dreamed up by philosophers,
that the dogma of popular sovereignty was an invitation to new forms
of despotism and cruelty, and that the reduction of the complexity
of human motives to the perfect equality of subjective preferences
and desires undermined any civilized conception of the "good life."
His liberalism went hand in hand with a fundamental rejection of
despotism in all its forms (like Montesquieu, Jouvenel decried the
despotic regime as "so monstrous that it is impossible to discuss [it]
without horror").[1] The spirit of Jouvenel's liberalism is perfectly
conveyed by Montesquieu's poignant remark in the second book
of *The Spirit of the Laws*: "Since despotism inflicts the most dreadful
evils upon human nature, anything that limits despotism is good."[2]

Jouvenel shared none of the doctrinaire propensities of modern political philosophy. He attempted to recover the latitude for political prudence that was part of the estimable legacy of the premodern Western political tradition. He therefore fully appreciated that there were a variety of legitimate nondespotic political forms, and he did not hesitate to write about the "aristocratic roots of liberty."[3] In his view, authentic liberty was the product of a centuries-old duel between "Power" and the "freeman."[4] Liberty depended on the self-assertion of genuinely independent citizens who were equally distant from the abuses of an "insolent plutocracy" and the slavishness of the "disinherited mass" (OP, 366). Jouvenel was thus the furthest thing from a dogmatic democrat, even if he would come to appreciate that democracy is an essential precondition for political liberty in the contemporary world.

Near the end of his life, Jouvenel wrote that the greatness of the West could be located in the fact that it was a civilization that had never known or justified despotism. *On Power: The Natural History of Its Growth* is the starting point for any analysis of Jouvenel's thought precisely because it provides a rich Jouvenelian account of how the modern West—the West that had done so much to estrange itself from its classical and Christian sources—became vulnerable to novel forms of despotism. The much-remarked pathos of the work derives from the fact that it was composed during Jouvenel's Swiss exile and is his first unflinching attempt to come to terms with the tragedy that had befallen liberal and Christian civilization. *On Power* is not Jouvenel's deepest or most theoretical work. But a case can be made for its fundamental importance. It has the virtue of rooting our understanding of the twentieth century in the larger adventure of modernity. The book's critique of the tyrannical possibilities inherent in democratic modernity is by no means original to him. Great nineteenth-century thinkers such as Tocqueville and Taine proceeded Jouvenel by a century in pointing out that "democracy . . . in the centralizing, pattern-making, absolutist shape which we have given to it is . . . the time of tyranny's incubation" (OP, 15). But Jouvenel renewed their insights in a particularly suggestive, even compelling manner. And his grand historical narrative on the fate of liberty in the modern world laid the groundwork for his more profoundly philosophical engagement with the limits of theoretical modernity in *Sovereignty: An Inquiry into the Political Good*.

On Power is a deeply personal book, despite its author's claim that he was providing a merely scientific or analytic account of the origins, nature, and growth of Power, of "l'ensemble des elements gouvernementaux."[5] The volume is a learned and anguished account of the process by which Western man succumbed to the pernicious temptation of a democratic "monocracy" (OP, 317). The "monocratic" or "monolithic" state is marked by the destruction of vigorous "social authorities" (OP, 143, 378–79) between the state and the individual, and the "absorption of law" (OP, 322) by a sovereign state that recognizes no moral authority outside itself. Some critics have mistakenly discerned in *On Power* a libertarian indictment of politics *tout court* or a romantic exercise in aristocratic or medieval nostalgia.[6] The Jouvenel of *On Power* was, however, neither a libertarian nor a romantic conservative. Rather, he is best understood as a proponent of "limited power" who drew on the best resources of classical, Christian, and liberal thought to renew a humane tradition of antidespotic thought. Even more than the constitutional "separation of powers," truly limited power depends on the existence of a range of "makeweights" or "countervailing powers"[7] with "sufficient character and energy" (OP, 318) to be able to check the despotic propensities of the state. Jouvenel willingly affirmed the legitimate authority of the lawful state but opposed any notion of a unified and unlimited imperium that usurped the responsibilities of the many forms of *Potestas* (the Romans' word for the power of official or established authorities) that could cross each other's paths in fruitful and invigorating ways (OP, 317). Whether it was a question of the Roman tribunate, the self-assertion of the politically responsible English aristocracy described by Montesquieu, the independent judicial bodies (parliaments) of the French old regime, or the syndicates and employers' associations of the modern capitalist state, a free society depends on the "various conglomerations of interests and loyalties which arise spontaneously in society and which Power seeks instinctively to dissolve" (OP, 317). Jouvenel did not deny that these social authorities can be oppressive in their own right. The state had a responsibility to check the abuses of the "barons" even as the "barons" kept the state from imposing unlimited domination. Jouvenel was convinced that no society of free men could dispense with these "precious bulwarks of liberty" (OP, 321) without inviting both political tyranny and the evisceration of the natural complexity of the social order. But the modern state had ruthlessly subordinated every social authority, every makeweight, to its lordship. And it had been aided in this process of usurpation by intellectually bankrupt doctrines of popular sovereignty that mistook the power of the people with its liberty, to paraphrase the great Montesquieu.[8] As a result of the monocratic ascendancy, democratic politics had become little more than a protracted struggle to control the commanding heights of an increasingly lawless state.

The natural law was the other imposing pillar of Jouvenel's "doctrine of limited power" (OP, 314–15). Jouvenel even went so far as to suggest that "the absence in society of any concrete authorities capable of restraining Power does not matter if Power itself makes humble submission before the abstract force of the natural law" (OP, 334). In Jouvenel's view, the "supremacy of law," of an unchanging standard above the will of men, "should be the great and central theme of all political science" (OP, 334). In *On Power*, Jouvenel affirmed that law and jurisprudence must ultimately be subordinated to morality, right reason, and the sovereignty of God. He freely appealed to the wisdom of Aristotle, St. Thomas, and Montesquieu and expressed his admiration for the antitotalitarian conception of law and social order that could be found in the great Catholic social encyclicals of the first part of the twentieth century (OP, 350–51). *On Power* is an act of intellectual recovery, an effort to expose the perniciousness of a view of man and society that reduces the human world to the ceaseless conflict of wills in a world dominated by the sole realities of the individual and the state.

"The Minotaur Presented"

Nowhere is *On Power*'s unforced combination of intellectual penetration and highly wrought pessimism about the political condition of contemporary man more apparent than in the remarkable opening chapter of the book ("The Minotaur Presented"). This chapter is the *cri du coeur* of a civilized European who has been forced by events to come to terms with the self-destructive impulses of Western civilization. But Jouvenel responded in a particularly impressive manner to the recent catastrophe. He was not content with merely exploring the contemporary sources of European militarism and totalitarianism. In his view, totalitarian tyranny and "total war" were the most recent and tragic manifestations of a broader pathology that had become ever more visible during the long march from feudal-medieval to modern democratic times. For all their murderous fury Hitler and the Nazis were only "the proximate cause" of the "total militarization" that would make everyone ("workmen, peasants, and women alike") and everything ("the factory, the harvest, even the dwelling house") a target in a war that unleashed deadly new terrors from the sky (all quotations from OP, 3–4). The prodigious energies of the modern state, this formidable "power house" (OP, 13) as Jouvenel called it, was the sine qua non for unleashing destruction on such a truly "unprecedented scale." Jouvenel thus came to place both totalitarianism and total war in the broader context of the inexorable growth of Power in modern times. They were the culmination of a more fundamental expansion of state power that first emerged during the "absolutist" period of the European old regime. As a result of these considerations Jouvenel turned his focus from the barbarism of the present to the relatively unappreciated historical origins of the modern state. Nor was his a merely historical or genealogical account.

Jouvenel came to formulate a "political metaphysic" (OP, 19) that he believed provided a deeper explanation for the assaults on liberty in his own time. At the root of the hypertrophy of the modern state lies the implacable hostility of the governing political authorities, in any time or place, to every institution, barrier, or claim that stands in their way. Power is the great leveler that sets out to curtail or eliminate every social authority that mediates between the individual and the state. Jouvenel came to see that "the struggle to magnify itself is of Power's essence" (OP, 7) and cannot be explained by accidental or ephemeral considerations. He argued that Power's ultimate, if never wholly acknowledged goal, is the complete atomization of society. In chapter 9 of *On Power* ("Power, Assailant of the Social Order") Jouvenel brilliantly chronicles the various "statocratic offenses" (OP, 177) that Power directed in turn against ancient clans, medieval barons, and modern capitalists. Here Jouvenel also appropriates Marx's arresting image of the state as a "boa constrictor" that ceaselessly closes in on every social authority or group that stands in its way.[9] "Where will it end?" Jouvenel asks with apprehension. His answer is disconcerting, to say the least. Power will only be satisfied, he suggests, by the "disappearance of every constraint which does not emanate from the state, and in the denial of every pre-eminence which is not approved by the state." The "predestined course" of the modern adventure, the culmination of Power's "natural history," is nothing less than "the rupture of every tie linking man and man." At the end of the journey, "the extremes of individualism and socialism meet" as men stand alone in "equal abasement before the power of their absolute master, the state" (all quotations from OP, 187).

To substantiate this paradoxical claim, Jouvenel devotes considerable space to exposing the underlying affinities and secret complicities between the unlimited ambitions of Power and every "democratic" justification of omnipotent authority exercised in the name of the people. Without such justifications, Power would find it much more difficult to achieve its goal. In this connection, Jouvenel also brings to light the essentially oligarchic character of Power (which can never entail the "rule of the people") and reveals how modern democracy masks Power's "egoism" even as it undermines those traditional institutions and social bodies that are the most important obstacles to the establishment of a "monolithic state" (OP, 322). Thus, while he begins with the deadly struggle between free and tyrannical regimes in the twentieth century, he soon turns his attention to the unceasing conflict between kings and barons in a medieval Europe where the state could hardly even be said to exist. This is not an exercise in "aristocratic nostalgia" but rather evidence of Jouvenel's determined effort to uncover the traditional sources of European liberty and to trace the hidden trajectory that led to the tragic twentieth century.

Like the Minotaur, the mythical half-bull, half-human creature that ravaged everything that entered its labyrinth on Crete, the modern state is a monstrous force, at best half human, that also requires periodic sacrifices to keep its fury at bay. But in Jouvenel's modern rendition there is no heroic Theseus on hand to destroy it or to deliver future generations from its wrath. Instead, democratic appeals to the "general will" and the "sovereignty of the people" only serve to "mask" Power's essentially antisocial ambitions and to justify its expansion (OP, 35–43, 279–81). In stark contrast, Jouvenel points out that the leading lights of the European old regime were exceedingly sensitive to the slightest royal encroachments on their liberties and privileges. But now that Power derives its legitimacy from the will of the people, intellectuals tend to confuse its self-serving justifications with genuine solicitude for the common good and are thus led to excuse its advances. Some of the most suggestive pages in *On Power* describe this sempiternal dialectic of "Thought and Power," which culminates in the shameful excuses of progressive intellectuals for some of the most tyrannical regimes in human history.[10] Philosophers too often dream of ideal republics "secured at the price of universal registration and wholesale regimentation." Constant had good reason, indeed, for mocking "the unphilosophical preference of the learned for authoritarian methods." Jouvenel suggests that that those who dedicate themselves to Thought are frequently attracted to what is simple and symmetrical at the expense of the inherent complexity and intractability of the human world. Modern intellectuals, in particular, take delight in "put[ting] into society's head" grand visions for the transformation of men and societies, visions that can only be actuated by "immense effort[s]" on the part of the state. "Even in giving battle to the actual incumbents of authority," they "are still working for authority's enlargement" (see OP, 149). Rare are those thinkers such as Proudhon, who presciently warned that modern democracy provides unprecedented opportunities for the enhancement of the imperium, for the satisfaction of the age-old ambitions of Power (OP, 14).

Throughout *On Power*, Jouvenel keeps his eyes clearly focused on "The Expansionist Character of Power," to cite the title of the book's seventh chapter. In that chapter, though, he modifies his unremittingly bleak portrait of Power without departing from the essentials of his analysis. Here he shows that he is no simple-minded antistatist by emphasizing the constructive social purposes that may be served by established political authorities. The "intoxicating pleasure of moving the pieces on the board of the social game" is inseparable from the "social virtues" regularly exhibited by legitimate and long-established political authorities (OP, 135). Jouvenel's ire therefore is directed less at the egoism of Power than at a misplaced idealism that allows governmental authorities to proceed with their depredations as long as they are said to serve ostensibly "social" purposes. In particular, modern thought has been all too eager to excuse Power's crimes when they are directed against "undemocratic" social authorities. It displays a misplaced, even "magical" (OP, 144) confidence in the state as the principal or only "repository of human hopes" (OP, 143). Above all, Jouvenel is an opponent of this incendiary mix of egoism and idealism which comes to the forefront in a democratic age. He sets out to "unmask" the humanitarian pretensions of the Minotaur in order to restore a salutary appreciation of Power's nature and limits.

The opening chapter of *On Power*, "The Minotaur Revisited" (OP, 3–16), bears a striking resemblance in its historical sweep to Tocqueville's "Author's Introduction" to volume I of *Democracy in America*. But if Tocqueville famously described the "democratic revolution" that relentlessly transformed the Christian European world from the twelfth century onward, Jouvenel examines the same period only to subordinate the rise of democracy or "the equality of conditions" to his theme of the expansion of centralized Power. To be sure, Tocqueville and Jouvenel are in full agreement about the essential connection between democracy and centralization.

They tell comparable stories, with reference to the same sequence of events. But in contrast to Tocqueville's account, Jouvenel deliberately makes the rise of democracy or the "equality of conditions" an episode in the larger history of Power. Democracy and totalitarianism become two essential but subordinate moments in the history of Power's inexorable growth. Both the strengths and weaknesses of *On Power* are tied to this singular preoccupation with the ravenous appetite of the Minotaur and the "political metaphysic" that explains it. If, as we shall argue, Jouvenel's analysis finally goes too far in downplaying the originality of totalitarian or ideological regimes, it is nonetheless a remarkably thoughtful attempt to show how the rise of totalitarianism is part of the larger historical dynamic of the Western world. As Dennis Hale and Marc Landy have argued, Jouvenel's "great contribution is to give totalitarianism a genealogy. In doing so, however, he has demonstrated the embarrassing fact that the totalitarian state, black sheep though it may be, is a legitimate member of the modern family of nations: not only does it have the same ancestors, it has many of the same family characteristics, even if in a distorted or exaggerated form."[11]

No account of modern politics should ignore the crucial role that war and "political rivalry" have played in fueling Power's relentless expansion.[12] The study of Power's growth necessarily entails the study of war (and vice versa). War, in fact, has been a central catalyst in transforming Power from a relatively "small scale affair" (OP, 7) under the feudal old regime to the quasi-total instrument of social transformation that it has become in a democratic age. Accordingly, the opening chapter of *On Power* provides an account both of the militarization of modern politics and of the ways in which the relentless centralization of Power in modern times has reinforced the warmaking capacities of the state. No society was or is immune from these developments, since free societies must to some extent emulate the methods of dictatorial ones if they are to survive in a dangerous world. Jouvenel describes a kind of prisoner's dilemma in which the most centralizing, tyrannical, and aggressive states set the tone for international—and, to an increasing and alarming extent, domestic—life. While Power has an inherent logic of its own, the rivalry of nations and peoples provides a powerful impetus and practical justification for the continuing enhancement of the military capacities of the state. War and Power conspire in a dizzying dialectic, one that reinforces the centralizing and despotic propensities of the modern state.

From the Feudal Order to the Modernizing State

Some critics have suggested that *On Power* presents an excessively romantic and stylized portrait of the Middle Ages.[13] There is some truth to this charge, but not much. Jouvenel's intention was not to present a comprehensive account of the strengths and weaknesses of the medieval social and political order. Rather, the Middle Ages provided him with an essential spiritual reference point, a moral-political lodestar indispensable for clarifying the defining features of the modern age. Just as Tocqueville believed that the new democratic dispensation could only truly be understood and evaluated in contrast to the "social whole" that he called aristocracy,[14] so Jouvenel was convinced that the Middle Ages could help clarify what was genuinely distinctive about the modern world. He had no illusions about the manifold injustices that characterized the medieval order or about its inability to adequately provide for the basic needs of ordinary human beings. But the undeniable virtues of medieval man—an abiding suspicion of every form of centralized control, a proud refusal to bow before illegitimate or arbitrary authority, humble deference to a moral law above the will of men—were in short supply in the contemporary world. Since Jouvenel had no reason to fear a medieval restoration, he did not dwell on the well-known injustices and inequalities that marred that essentially libertarian civilization. In any case, the partisans of a vulgar understanding of "enlightenment" endlessly trumpeted this version of events. They disparaged the moral and cultural inheritance of the European past as hopelessly mired in fear, superstition, and despotism. Jouvenel cannot be faulted for refusing to participate in that particular game.

If Jouvenel is more emphatically critical of the second phase of the old regime—the period of "absolutist" monarchy associated with centralizing rulers such as Louis XIV—it is precisely because this period saw a dangerous amplification of the state's capacity to make war and to restrict the traditional liberties of its people. On the eve of the French Revolution, Louis XVI had 180,000 men-at-arms compared to the paltry 12,000 troops that French king Charles VII managed to assemble during his reign in the fifteenth century (OP, 9). The centralizing monarchs of Europe had come to "acquire" the "legislative capacity" of the state—an assumption of power "unknown to the Middle Ages" (OP, 8)—and did not hesitate to use their new authority to impose onerous new taxes on an already excessively burdened society. In the seventeenth century these efforts were met with fierce resistance from both aristocrats and the people, a resistance that led to revolutions in Naples and England and to the revolt of the Fronde during the minority of Louis XIV (OP, 8). But the modernizing state—whether relatively "liberal" as in England or "absolutist" as in France—continued to convert its newfound wealth into state power and increasingly deadly displays of military strength. The expansion of centralized Power and the augmentation of the warmaking capacities of the state were two aspects of the same process of modernization. This frightful growth in the military power of European states alarmed the perceptive Montesquieu. Writing in *The Spirit of the Laws* in 1748, he warned that if this process were left unchecked, civilized Europeans risked "becom[ing] like Tartars" (quoted in OP, 9). Montesquieu was one of the first major European thinkers to raise the specter of a new kind of "civilized barbarism."

In a Tocquevillian spirit, Jouvenel emphasized the continuities between the "absolutism" of the old regime in its final, centralizing period, and the worst excesses of modern revolutionary and democratic politics. Pierre Hassner has succinctly formulated the essential insight of this position: "[R]ather than breaking the absolutism of the state," the French Revolution "further concentrated power in the hands of the state—a work that would be pushed even further by Napoleon."[15] If Jouvenel emphasized the most problematic features of "absolutism," it is because these aspects of the old order were linked with a whole new series of "democratic" pathologies. To be sure, Jouvenel acknowledged the great benefits that accompanied the rise of centralized monarchy. "To say that the monarchy did no more than increase the size of armies would be ridiculous. That it established internal order, that it protected the weak against the strong, that it raised the community's standard of life, that it conferred great benefits on industry, commerce, and agriculture—all that is well known" (OP, 9). But as with his treatment of the Middle Ages, Jouvenel refuses to dwell on what is already well known. He instead warns his readers that viewing the state primarily as a social benefactor only increases the possibility that it will abuse its authority by perpetrating new usurpations. Following Tocqueville, Jouvenel points out the inherent connections between a "providential" or "tutelary" understanding of the state and new forms of "democratic despotism." We are now in a better position to understand why Jouvenel was slow to acknowledge the benefits of centralization, the goods served by the emerging modern state. But even with this caveat, one may observe that in this regard he is less just than Tocqueville, who never lost sight of the justice of the democratic dispensation.

The Triumph of Democracy and the Coming of Tyranny

The absolute monarchy was the period of transition from a relatively decentralized medieval order, marked by ceaseless contestation between kings and barons, popes and emperors, to a more consistently modern form of politics and society. But it was absolutist only in contrast to the much more diffuse politics of the Middle Ages. For while the old regime placed many "heavy burdens" on European peoples, the absolutist monarchies could only dream of establishing conscription and a permanent and regularized system of taxation (OP, 10). It was really the displacement of the old regime by a new democratic order that allowed "these burdens" to "grow heavier" under an allegedly "up-to-date regime" (OP, 10). In *Les origines de la France contemporaine*, Taine memorably described conscription and universal suffrage as "twin brothers," the ballot always accompanied by the soldier's knapsack. The great French historian famously predicted that the twentieth century would witness the perversion of science at the service of a "retrograde movement towards a barbarous and instinctual egotism" (cited in OP, 10–11), a retrogression made possible by the triumph of the modern plebiscitarian state.

Writing at the end of the Second World War, Jouvenel remarks that events had "surpassed even the imagination of Taine" (OP, 11). Unimaginable millions of soldiers and civilians had been killed or wounded in a "total war" that engendered the frenzied mobilization of men and resources on all sides. In *On Power* Jouvenel feared that democracy had only succeeded in ushering in a new age of barbarism. "We are ending where the savages began" (OP, 11). In 1945, Jouvenel was far from hopeful about the prospects for the restoration of a European order that would master its social passions and reestablish regimes of balanced liberty.

There were quite plausible reasons, of course, for Jouvenel's near despondency about the outcome of the modern adventure. The Middle Ages knew all manner of injustice. But modernity saw the rise of new social doctrines that would provide ideological validation for the wholesale murder of tens of millions of human beings solely because of their suspect racial, class, or social origins. It was only in a modern or "enlightened" age that intellectuals would come to repudiate the very idea of a moral law independent of the will of men and nations. The absolutist monarchies of the seventeenth and eighteenth centuries did much to undermine those social authorities whose glory had been their fierce determination to keep the usurpations of Power in check. But the theorists of the old regime never failed to affirm the limits inherent in every exercise of earthly authority. In the sharpest contrast, the modern state derived its legitimacy from a conception of "sovereignty" that recognized no limitation on the authority of the state other than that authorized by the "general will" or required by "the greatest good of the greatest number." This assuredly needed to be noted and explored by any friend of European liberty.

The Pathos of On Power

If the final period of the old regime provided the modern "power house" with some formidable weapons, it was modern democracy that gave it its "claws and talons" (OP, 14). It was democracy that declared that the general will was the sole and sufficient source of political legitimacy. It was the democratic state that established "an inquisitorial mechanism of taxation" (OP, 15), as well as the mass or "mechanized" party that would become the chosen instrument of totalitarian control (OP, 15, 299–306). Democracy also prepared the way for the "ideological" manipulation of men's souls through the establishment of a state monopoly over education. According to Jouvenel, even the modern police regime grew in the "shadow of democracy" (OP, 15). The ancient régime never knew such evils. For while it was by no means free from the ordinary defects of human nature or from that will to power that afflicts the human soul in every historical and cultural setting, its leading spirits were sensitive to the slightest encroachments by Power. They were not taken in by the modern sophistries that served to justify the unjustifiable. And "the consecrated King of the Middle Ages was a Power as tied down and as little arbitrary as we can conceive" (OP, 33).

It was only with the rise of modern theories of sovereignty, theories that denied a superintending principle above the human will, that Power was able to become a complete law unto itself. Prominent postrevolutionary liberal theorists such as Constant, Royer-Collard, and Guizot would direct the full force of their minds and eloquence against the modern defenses of unlimited power put forth by such diverse thinkers as Hobbes, Spinoza, Helvétius, Malby, and, in a more qualified manner, Rousseau (OP, 39–47). These chastened liberals tried to reconnect modern liberty to traditional understandings of the restraints that must bind any exercise of the human will. Jouvenel endorses these efforts to unite the essential moral insight of the old regime with the liberties of the modern world. The fourth chapter of this book ("The Spirit of Sovereignty and the Regulated Will") will examine Jouvenel's impressive effort in *Sovereignty* to renew this noble tradition of liberal theorizing.

In the end, however, *On Power*'s effort to formulate a doctrine of "limited power" was undermined by Jouvenel's rather debilitating fear of the ultimate "ubiquity" (OP, 16) and irresistibility of the Minotaur. In the dramatic final pages of his introduction to *On Power*, Jouvenel raises the specter of new barbarian cruelties, of wars and tyrannies that would finally unmask the "benevolent . . . face" (OP, 16) that had for too long allowed Power to do its work unimpeded. At the same time, he denies that he is "setting [himself] up as an enemy of the growth of Power and of the distension of the state" (OP, 16). He unfurls a forceful jeremiad even as he denies that he is doing so. Rather he insists that his book is a scientific analysis of "the reasons why, and the way in which, Power grows in society." He seems to be unable to encapsulate his own aim or achievement. I do not mean to suggest that these tensions or possible contradictions in any way suggest dishonesty or bad faith on Jouvenel's part. Rather, it is my contention that when confronting the fateful millennial distension of the Minotaur, Jouvenel was unable to fully integrate moral evaluation and lived experience with the "scientific" analysis of social phenomena. He partially succumbed to pathos even as he exaggerated the disinterested or "scientific" character of his own analysis. More strikingly, he couldn't decide if the specter haunting the West was soft despotism (the "social protectorate" as he called it),[16] since the "desire" of modern man's "hearts is social security" (OP, 16), or a new age of totalitarian cruelties where hardness would be the order of the day.

We have already concurred that it was quite proper for Jouvenel to place totalitarianism within the broader context of an analysis of modernity and modernization. As we will explore at greater length in chapter 3, Jouvenel's analysis has the particular merit of exposing the limits of that "destructive metaphysic" that "refused to see in society anything but the state and the individual." This misplaced metaphysic, rooted in the erroneous assumptions of "individualist rationalism," helped undermine the various spiritual and social authorities that "enframe, protect, and control the life of man" (all quotations from OP, 417). It thus played a decisive role in preparing the way for new forms of collectivist tyranny. Moreover, Jouvenel's discussion has the additional virtue of highlighting the indebtedness of totalitarian regimes and ideologies to various illiberal or "absolutist" doctrines of sovereignty. Even if democratic and totalitarian regimes are radically opposed in practice, both "clearly state that human beings are sovereign over themselves and create themselves in history."[17]

Social Protectorate or Totalitarian Despotism?

Unfortunately, Jouvenel's salutary effort to locate both democracy and modern tyranny within the common nexus of modernity were ultimately compromised by an unfortunate tendency to conflate the social protectorate with ideological despotism. Too often Jouvenel writes as if these were merely two forms of a unitary or undifferentiated "totalitarian democracy."[18] At a minimum, he failed to adequately distinguish between real and metaphorical expressions of totalitarianism. The contemporary reader cannot help but balk at the inference that the welfare state and the Gulag archipelago emanate from the same fundamental impulse in the modern heart and mind. Jouvenel's discussion of these matters lacks rhetorical precision and the requisite degree of analytic clarity. In the end, he cannot quite decide if totalitarianism or the welfare state, barbarous cruelties or timid and hedonistic self-satisfaction, "marks the culmination of the history of the West" (OP, 16). As even a sympathetic critic has pointed out in a discerning article that attempts to restore the French political philosopher to his rightful place as a "precusor of the critique of totalitarianism,"[19] Jouvenel almost always identified "totalitarian democracy" with that "'tutelary despotism' to which Tocqueville thought democracy risked succumbing if it accentuated its egalitarianism to the detriment of the sentiment of liberty."[20] This identification of totalitarianism with "soft" or "tutelary" despotism is more partial or one-sided than simply wrong. Nevertheless, conflating hard and soft despotism misconstrues the nature of the evil that was the true scourge of the twentieth century. As Raymond Aron has perceptively stated, the despotisms that would leave their terrible mark on the twentieth century were "violent and ideocratic and only secondarily tutelary" in character.[21] *On Power* displays an insufficient appreciation of this incontrovertible fact.

The desire for "social security" has only an incidental connection to the rise of the modern totalitarian state in the proper, specific sense of the term: the two temporarily coincided in the first half of the twentieth century, when Europeans found themselves exhausted by what Aron has suggestively called "wars in chain reaction."[22] The humanitarian ethos of the modern welfare state, whatever its limits, is fundamentally incompatible with "the organization of enthusiasm"[23] that defines a revolutionary movement or regime. In addition, Jouvenel's argument does not really begin to anticipate the spiritual condition of postmodern Europe, which is marked by a hedonistic calculus that threatens to undermine the political virtues and has given rise to a process of humanitarian "depoliticization" that is the inverse of the "superpoliticization" unleashed by European totalitarianism.[24] This comparative neglect of the depoliticizing features of modern life is surprising on the part of a thinker who so admired Rousseau's "Discourse on the Arts and Sciences" and who wrote about it with evident intelligence and discernment.[25] In that seminal work of European political philosophy, Rousseau famously exclaimed that the progress of the arts and sciences would bring in its wake everything "except morals and Citizens."[26]

On Power: *Its Achievement and Limits*

It is true: *On Power* provides a remarkable and incisive analysis of the political condition of modern man. It articulates a penetrating defense of "limited power" against the despotism implicit in certain modern understandings of sovereignty. Jouvenel's stated aim of unmasking and demystifying the democratic illusions that have fuelled the march of the Minotaur is a wholly admirable one. But Jouvenel was finally too intent on telling the story of a tragedy to make the kinds of careful, calibrated distinctions that are essential to a balanced political science that wishes to preserve liberty in a democratic age. For all its historical and philosophical penetration, *On Power* fails to put forward a political science that can guide prudent men in the arduous task of domesticating the Minotaur. Perhaps this failure is the result of the fact that at the time he composed his great work, Jouvenel was genuinely convinced that the Minotaur was a quasi-natural force almost wholly beyond the control of human beings. Oscillating between moral evaluation and a natural history of the Minotaur, *On Power* illuminates a great deal even if it fails to be fully convincing.

Jouvenel's later and considerably less anguished books and essays are much more successful in integrating the humane art of liberty with a philosophical and scientific analysis of the nature of Power. In his greatest work of political philosophy, *Sovereignty* (1955), and in such illuminating essays from the following decade as "On the Evolution of Forms of Government," "The Principate," and "The Means of Contestation,"[27] Jouvenel succeeded in looking at Power "stereoscopically" (OP, 314), both as a profound moral and social necessity and as a "potential social menace" (OP, 314). He never repudiated *On Power's* fundamental insight that the ideological allure of democracy and socialism had made modern man dangerously complacent before the usurpations of Power. But these later works present a more adequate and constructive account of the moral purposes served by public authority. They do so without in any way abandoning Jouvenel's abiding concern with the importance of limiting and checking Power. These writings do more justice to the intrinsic dignity of the political vocation and the inherent nobility of citizenship and statesmanship. Jouvenel no longer treats Power as a monstrous force largely unamenable to prudent intervention by men. As a result, he was in a better position to address the problem of Power without succumbing to excessive pathos or debilitating fear.

"The Principate": Toward a New Constitutionalism

In "The Principate,"[28] which dates from 1965, Jouvenel continued to express serious reservations about the expansion of the size and scope of government as well as deep forebodings about the remarkable prestige of "princely" or executive power in the contemporary world. He remained faithful to the enduring insight of Constant and other nineteenth-century constitutionalists that "the proclamation of the sovereignty of the people was in itself no guarantee against *dominatio*."[29] But he was no longer content with merely lamenting the extension of state power, and he resigned himself to the dominant role the state would continue to play as the "representative" instrument of civil society. In this new view, the old constitutionalism associated with the political science of John Locke no longer resonated with a society where the state is a principal agent of social movement and change.[30] Good government no longer consists of an executive faithfully applying "sensible rules" drawn up by an elected legislature.[31] Instead, every government is now obliged to formulate *policies* that attempt to shape the direction of society and to promote socially desirable goals.[32] The modern prince is less the executor of laws than a "field commander" who relies on his civil service to conduct "operations with a given goal, taking the initiatives and decisions which seem necessary, adjusting measures to circumstances."[33] Jouvenel fully appreciated that this essentially *teleocratic* or goal-driven approach to politics poses terrible dangers to the regime of liberty.[34] Yet he also came to believe that it offers unique opportunities for devising a "new constitutionalism" that allows the state to "acquire the natural complexity of what it absorbs."[35] A complex bureaucratic state that allows senior civil servants to exercise political prudence and to check the concentration of power in the hands of a single ruler could serve as a "corrective to caeserism rather than an instrument of it."[36] The cultivation of "makeweights" or "countervailing powers" within the bureaucracy is, of course, no substitute for commonly agreed upon *principles* that are the ultimate source of limitations on the abuse of government power. But the decline of traditional social authorities and the weakened influence of natural law thinking in the second half of the twentieth century led Jouvenel to advocate a new constitutionalism that did not depend on a return to a social order or moral-philosophical consensus that showed little sign of reviving. He in no way abandoned his commitment to the "doctrine of limited power," but he willingly modified his means in light of changing circumstances and a revised estimation of the prospects for the revival of traditional constitutionalism. Jouvenel came to accept the state and civil society *as they were*. His hope now rested in a new doctrine of countervailing powers that might turn modern statism against itself.

In *Sovereignty*, Jouvenel brilliantly argued that the offices of *rex* and *dux*, of founder and stabilizer, are inherent in political leadership as such. In the third chapter of that work ("The Office of Leadership and the Office of Adjustment")[37] he highlighted two famous images, the one of Bonaparte inspiriting his soldiers at the bridge at Arcola and the other of St. Louis under the oak of Vincennes calming down those who approached him.[38] For Jouvenel, these images were illustrative of two distinct but complementary dimensions of political life. A politics that remained true to the social nature of man must learn to unite innovation and conservation, founding and stabilizing, in a manner that does justice to the requirements of the common good. A truly capacious conception of statesmanship should have room for both the active prince who agitates and stirs the political community and the sta-

bilizing prince who moderates disputes and restores social affections. Yet modern politics emphasizes movement or action to the
detriment of conciliation and stabilization. Public opinion responds
to the charismatic leader who moves men to great actions and largely
ignores the need for leadership that aims to preserve the framework of civil society and a humanizing sense of continuity with the
past.

In "The Principate," Jouvenel self-consciously builds on his
earlier analysis of leadership and adjustment in *Sovereignty*. He en-
visions a constitutionalism whereby the executive largely leaves the
task of stimulating movement or innovation to the various "barons" within the civil service of the modern bureaucratic state. Rather
than stirring up already excessively impassioned men, the executive would be "he, who, in the midst of movement provided by
others, appeases anxieties, stabilizes, reassures, is in one word the
guarantor."[39] Jouvenel's "new constitutionalism" would not only
provide functional restraints on government by establishing checks
and balances within the bureaucracy, but it would strike at the
essentially Caesarian conception of executive power that has come
to dominate the theory and practice of modern politics.

Thus we see that one should not drive a wedge between
Jouvenel's analyses of Power in his 1945 classic and his later political writings. Whether speaking in a more pathetic or measured
voice, whether recoiling from or largely accommodating himself
to the extension of state power in modern times, Jouvenel never
lost sight of the "precious" and "precarious" character of human
liberty.[40] He remained firmly committed to limiting power even if
he later resigned himself to the increasingly dominant role of the

state in modern democratic societies. In both his earlier and later phases Jouvenel refused to accommodate himself to the "intellectual vogue of the Principate."[41] He continued to resist every manifestation of the Caesarism that was the deadly enemy of constitutionalism in all its forms. For that reason alone, *On Power* remains an indispensable cornerstone in the Jouvenelian intellectual edifice.

CHAPTER THREE

BEYOND THE PRISON OF THE COROLLARIES: LIBERTY AND THE COMMON GOOD

CONTEMPORARY ACADEMIC POLITICAL theory, especially in the United States, is dominated by a largely sterile debate between liberals and communitarians. Academic liberals affirm the moral autonomy of the individual and the priority of rights over a commonly shared understanding of the good life. To a remarkable degree, they take for granted the moral preconditions of a free society—those habits, mores, and shared beliefs that allow for the responsible exercise of individual liberty. Raymond Aron's forceful retort to Hayek applies equally to other currents of academic liberal theory: they "presuppose, as already acquired, results which past philosophers considered as the primary objects of political action."[1] Contemporary liberals fail to see that "*a society must first be, before it can be free.*"[2]

Communitarians, in contrast, insist that human freedom must be nurtured in the context of a community marked by shared values and aspirations. On closer inspection, however, most communitarians turn out to be political liberals with a bad conscience: they are more or less conventional liberals who regret the individualism of a market society and yearn for the communal warmth and participatory politics that supposedly characterized an earlier era of "republican" politics. With the discrediting of Marxism in the late twentieth century, communitarianism allowed intellectuals to distance themselves from liberal capitalism while avoiding any open identification with socialist ideology. Rarely, however, do communitarians endorse those tough-minded political measures (e.g., support for the traditional family, public encouragement of religion, unequivocal opposition to abortion on demand) that would be necessary to sustain traditional moral communities against the pressures deriving from rights-based jurisprudence and the ethos of personal liberation.[3] The much trumpeted liberal-communitarian debate turns out to be, for the most part, an in-house controversy among those who refuse to question either the core theoretical assumptions of modernity or the reigning prejudices of the academic class.

The political reflection of Bertrand de Jouvenel provides a way out of this impasse. He was, broadly speaking, a "conservative liberal" in the tradition of Tocqueville. In his view, liberty truly worthy of the name cannot be based upon chimerical assumptions about the individual or collective "sovereignty" of man. Human liberty unfolds within a natural order of things that human beings did not create and to which they owe humble deference. A true conception of human dignity depends on a humanizing recognition of one's debts as well as a free acceptance of our obligations to others. Radical individualism is not only based on a false understanding of human nature but has deeply pernicious social consequences. It acts as an acid that erodes those intermediate social groups between the state and the individual which rein in the human will and check the insatiable growth of state power. In light of these considerations, Jouvenel rejects those libertarian moral premises common to almost all currents of contemporary political thought. But he also refuses to succumb to traditionalist complacency or to irresponsible nostalgia for the "lost treasure" of classical republicanism.[4] He accepts the inevitability and even the desirability of modern liberty while indicting the failure of modern theory to give a satisfying account of human experience.

Jouvenel is one of a series of important twentieth-century thinkers to renew "the quarrel of the ancients and the moderns." Leo Strauss primarily understood this great quarrel as a struggle between two conflicting philosophical conceptions of politics, human nature, and the whole of things.[5] Jouvenel does not ignore the philosophical dimensions of the quarrel but finally is more concerned with the differences between ancient and modern conceptions of liberty. He is less concerned with the status of the theoretical life than with the moral and political effects of ancient and modern conceptions of human nature and social order.

Jouvenel writes not as a partisan of classical philosophy, but rather as a modern man searching for spiritual and intellectual resources to sustain human liberty and dignity in new circumstances. In his view, these resources are by and large not to be found in modern political philosophy. In particular, he believes that no human community can avoid confronting the question of the common good—the question of how human beings ought to order their lives together. Classical philosophy was right to make this question the centerpiece of its political reflection. But Jouvenel also appreciates that any conception of the common good articulated in modern circumstances must accommodate the dynamic and heterogeneous character of the open society. A liberal society allows human beings the freedom to regularly introduce new initiatives and actions. Any effort to block new initiatives leads to social petrification and to the stultifying repression of human nature.

In Jouvenel's view, social dynamism is ultimately rooted in the spontaneity of human nature itself—in what Jouvenel calls "the inevitable diversity of men" (s, 158). All of Jouvenel's work returns to this central question: Can the indispensable notion of the common good be freed from those corollaries (i.e., smallness, homogeneity, resistance to innovation and foreign ideas, insistence on the community's immutability in order to maintain its harmony) in which classical political philosophy enframed it (see s, 147–48)? Can modern man draw on the wisdom of classical political philosophy without succumbing to a republican or communitarian nostalgia that at best romanticizes the harsh realities of the closed city and at worst gives rise to new, distinctively modern forms of tyranny? These are among the fundamental questions raised in Jouvenel's engagement of the problem of liberty and the common good.

Ancient and Modern Liberty

All of Jouvenel's work is a reflection on what the great postrevolutionary French liberal thinker Benjamin Constant called the "liberty of the ancients and the moderns."[6] In his famous essay of that name, originally published in 1819, Constant argued that the ancients were concerned nearly exclusively with public liberty, with collective deliberation within the public square, to the almost complete exclusion of individual liberty. Modern liberty, on the other hand, upholds the rights of the individual and treats political liberty as an instrumental means for the preservation of individual rights.[7] Constant admired the grandeur of the ancients but was repelled by their almost complete lack of an interior life, the absence of self-consciousness, with all the internal divisions that accompany it. The agonistic life of the ancient citizen, centered narrowly on public deliberations and military struggles, belongs to the glorious prehistory of the human race. Constant tried to neutralize nostalgia for ancient liberty by dismissing it as an anachronism, but he also thought contemporary Europeans and Americans should continue to admire its greatness and appeal to its public-spiritedness as a correction to the excessive individualism of modern times.[8]

In his own manner, Jouvenel is a friend of modern liberty and of the open or progressive society. But he is less convinced than is his great predecessor that the classical emphasis on the common good is a mere anachronism. His work explores the possibility of freeing the common good from "the prison of the corollaries," from its historical identification with the above-mentioned categories of ancient thought. He believes this is necessary because once human beings have left behind the primitive community or the closed classical city, they are committed to a "prodigious adventure which cannot but bring grave disappointments in its train" (s, 166). This worldwide adventure is marked by a great proliferation of individual initiatives that leaves "progress" in its wake.

Still, Jouvenel learned from Rousseau that the development of civilization does not necessarily entail human happiness or moral progress. Any genuine political community depends on "mutual trust" and social friendship. And both of these are undermined by progress, or by democratic individualism. Modern progress unfolds at the expense of strong "bilateral affinities" (see PT, 70) and the moral harmony that marks primitive ("face-to-face") human communities. Under the conditions of modernity, the self is no longer quite at home in the human world, and the "anxious ego" confronts the indifferent sea of "otherdom." In *The Pure Theory of Politics*, Jouvenel suggestively remarks that the modern novel is a record of the ego's unnerving confrontation with a hostile external world (PT, 80–81). Collectivist politics and nostalgia for primitive community are thus understandable—if terribly wrongheaded—responses to modernity's profound spiritual dislocations. And a liberalism that identifies political and technological progress with moral improvement mistakes the nature of man. Such a liberalism cannot adequately account for the spiritual discontents that accompany the modern adventure.

The Problem of the Common Good

This is not all. In contrast to the dominant currents of modern thought, Jouvenel refuses to jettison the idea of the common good. In his view, however, the common good is not an a priori "platonic ideal" to be imposed on a society by its rulers. That is the surest road to tyranny. Instead, the common good is best understood as a question that arises naturally in response to the exercise of authority in any political community, at any time or place. Jouvenel develops this essential insight in the opening pages of *Sovereignty*:

> Every man who finds himself dressed in the smallest degree of authority over another (and that is the case with even the least important citizen of a republic) is bound to form some conception of the good which he hopes to achieve by the exercise of the power which is his. Will he use it, small though it may be, despotically by making the good sought only his own good, or will he use it properly in the interest of a good which is in some way common? (s, xxv)

To reinforce his point, Jouvenel cites Aristotle's *Nicomachean Ethics* (Book 8, 1160b): "The despot is he who pursues his own good." The proponents of radical individualism, of individual autonomy, share despotism's basic premise that there can be no good held in common by human beings. This leads to an impoverished conception of political life as at best a series of negotiated settlements in an ongoing war rather than to a salutary understanding of politics as a common endeavor for pursuing shared goals and goods that transcend political partnership.

In chapters 7 and 8 of *Sovereignty*, titled "The Problem of the Common Good" and "Of Social Friendship," respectively, Jouvenel further clarifies his understanding of the common good. Most Anglo-American political theorists would be surprised by Jouvenel's discussion. It focuses on widespread social attitudes and habits— what the French moralists referred to as *moeurs*—and avoids putting forward any abstract rights-based "theory of justice."[9] In Jouvenel's presentation, the common good is tied to the strength of the social tie itself. The "social tie" is a good in itself, since society is an absolute precondition for the individual's pursuit of his personal goods. "No man is an island unto himself," and few goods are simply individual or private in character. The common good also depends on the warmth of friendship felt by one citizen for another, on the cultivation of civic and personal affections. Finally, the common good relies on social stability, the assurance that each has of the predictability of another's conduct. It is impossible to conceive of a society without trust, and human life itself is unlivable without the predictability that trust makes possible. Jouvenel is one with Rousseau and the classical political philosophers in affirming that "the essential function of public authorities" is "to increase the mutual trust prevailing at the heart of the social whole" (s, 147).

But the emphasis on "moral harmony within the city"—the "ruling preoccupation of Plato and Rousseau" (s, 147)—has been traditionally identified with certain corollaries that are in tension with the defense of an open, heterogeneous society. Jouvenel seems to be committed to incompatible goals: the open society characterized by numerous, overlapping individual initiatives, and the moral harmony of a political community that actively cultivates mutual affections. This conundrum is never fully resolved or overcome by Jouvenel, nor does he promise to do so.[10] But he suggests a way to mitigate it in his remarkable discussion of the aforementioned prison of the corollaries.

Jouvenel recognizes that the corollaries (again: small size and population, cultural and social homogeneity, resistance to innovation, and insistence on social immutability) "condemn the whole historical process, which is marked by just these four things" (s, 148). That is, the movement of Western history finds its promptings, according to Jouvenel, in the diversity inherent in human nature. The classical effort to establish and maintain the closed, immutable city thus appears to be profoundly unnatural.

But Jouvenel insists that such a conclusion is precipitous. These corollaries may be necessary means to maintain the social tie and to cultivate the affections that are profoundly natural to man. If this is the case, then nature is divided against itself. It therefore is with some hesitancy that Jouvenel sets out to liberate the common good and social friendship from the prison of the corollaries. He never forgets that it would be "presumptuous" to dismiss these corollaries out of hand. A careful reflection on the preconditions of civic affection as well as an attentive regard for the profound meditations of Plato and Rousseau remind us that it is natural for men to try to maintain "an inner harmony" (s, 149), which is already present in any community. It is natural for human beings to resist changes that undermine the integrity of the social bond itself. Once undermined or lost, it is extremely difficult to reconstruct the fragile ties that bind members of a community to each other.

In this connection, Jouvenel places great emphasis on what he calls "the dimensional law."[11] The larger and more complex the society, the weaker those bilateral affinities will be that connect individuals to one another. He fully appreciates that "the climate of trust prevailing in the various groups may never be felt again after the group's enlargement" (s, 150). Plato and Rousseau were right to question whether a recognizable political community could exist in a large extended territory ("Babylon")—whether such a community could be held together short of a repressive system of laws.

Nevertheless, in full awareness of these important considerations, Jouvenel sides with the open society against the harmonious city. To be sure, he acknowledges the conservative claim that "trustfulness within the group is not only a moral good in itself" but is a "condition of the various advantages which the members of society confer on each other" (s, 150). But he finally comes down on the side of societal enlargement because the alternative would be a constant repression of the spontaneous stirrings of human nature. He suggests that trustfulness would be a "sterile thing" if it could "be maintained only at the cost of suppressing the individual initiatives making for new relationships" (s, 150). Human beings would then purchase stability at a terrible cost to their humanity and individuality. Jouvenel believes that there is something inhuman about a singular preference for civic harmony even at the expense of new relationships and initiatives. He points out that Western philosophers were really only able to apply this "doctrine of unchangeableness" (s, 150) to mythical communities (such as the political community of the *Republic*) located in the distant past or unforeseeable future. Real political communities always need to wrestle with the problem of reconciling "reliability with freedom and change" (PT, 69). No human society can ever escape the ravages of time or forever resist the inherent diversity of human nature. The ideal of the closed immutable city was utopian even within the context of "ancient liberty."

Yet Jouvenel questions whether it is wise simply to dispense with these corollaries. He is torn between "a reasonably clear idea of the common good" and the "unacceptable" character of the corollaries that seem to be logically deduced from them (s, 151). He appreciates the force of the objection raised by the "good citizen" who fears that by jettisoning the corollaries that make civic harmony possible—the strong affinities that actually exist in traditional society—the advocates of the open society are trading uncertain hopes and promises for new and untried human relations. As a result of these considerations, Jouvenel cautions against a too precipitous "escape" from "the prison of the corollaries." He warns that a violent overthrow of these "four walls" could "bring down the whole building" (s, 152). How then does one preserve moral cohesion and social friendship without trying to put a stop to the historical adventure that is rooted in the spontaneity of human nature itself?

Jouvenel provocatively suggests that the common good cannot be the only or principal "star and compass" for an open, dynamic society. Social friendship and mutual trust must be reconceived as "the essential framework, or the network of roads" (s, 154) that each member of society uses for his own ends. The magistrate has the responsibility of repairing these roads, of maintaining common civic affections. But it would be contrary to human nature and the profound tendencies of modern society to forbid the individual's use of these roads altogether. Statesmen must continually attend to the common good in order to prevent the fraying of the social structure, while allowing reasonable space for the "free development of the various interests which form in society" (s, 155). A properly liberal conception of the common good must respect the autonomy of civil society without reducing the common good to the sum total of individual wills and initiatives. This is easier said than done, however. It appears as if Jouvenel has merely restated the problem of the common good in a liberal society rather than providing guidance as to how to promote or preserve it. But in this case, clarity about the nature of the problem may be the beginning of wisdom.

Jouvenel is particularly critical of the "Rousseauan" identification of social friendship with Sparta, "the most unvarying Greek community" (s, 156). The Spartan cultivation of civic conformity—and its accompanying militarization of human life—"directly conflicts with the development of human personality." More originally, he argues that both "reactionary" and "revolutionary" efforts to organize conformity in modern times have been consciously or unconsciously inspired by the Spartan model. He mocks modern revolutionaries who place a "revolutionary mask" over the most "routine-loving and ignorant conservatism" (s, 156). The error of the "Laecodomonian" party from Plato and Xenophon to Plutarch and Rousseau was to confuse social friendship with "mere similarity" (s, 156), and thus to forget that individuality must play a role in the articulation of a genuinely humane common good.

Jouvenel's emphasis in chapter 8 of *Sovereignty* on the reactionary and anachronistic character of modern revolutionary politics is indebted to Constant's critique of the French revolutionary cult of ancient liberty: it also closely resembles Karl Popper's assimilation (in *The Open Society and Its Enemies*) of Plato and Marx as philosophical enemies of liberty.[12] In my view, Jouvenel's argument suffers from many of the same defects as Constant's and Popper's. It conflates the theoretical and practical judgment of Plato by ignoring his fundamental reservations about the adequacy of any and all political orders.[13] By inordinately emphasizing the anachronistic character of revolutionary aspirations, it understates the profoundly modern theoretical underpinnings of totalitarian tyranny. In fairness to Jouvenel, however, his "Spartan argument" is meant to supplement *Sovereignty*'s overall emphasis on the connection between twentieth-century tyranny and the modern emancipation of the will.[14] Jouvenel's analysis of modern tyranny draws on three distinct lines of argument that to a large extent capture and reflect the ambiguity of the revolutionary phenomena: in *On Power* he stresses the imperial character of Power itself, defined by a ceaseless desire to expand and the various instrumentalities governments have devised to effect their will; in *Sovereignty* he analyzes the at once anachronistic and hypermodern character of revolutionary movements and totalitarian regimes.

Jouvenel argued that while social friendship is a great and valuable good, systematic efforts to promote it are generally beyond the competence of the magistrate. He was well aware that the statesman must be attentive to any fundamental threat to the integrity of the social order. He therefore despised a facile progressivism that took the achievements of civilized order for granted. Civilization is, first and foremost, an inheritance to be protected. And political art is "necessary to its support and development" (s, 136). But Jouvenel provides few concrete suggestions on how the magistrate might promote social friendship in the open society.[15] He suggests that in a highly developed society, law and general feelings of universal obligation rooted in religion and philosophy will tend to replace personal sympathy and affection as the major sources of civic trust (s, 158). Modern societies will tend to acquire universal bases, in Jouvenel's view. Jouvenel's reservations about the closed city are undoubtedly tied to his Christian recognition of the essential equality of persons as children of God and his personal adherence to the universal human community that is the Roman Catholic Church.

Jouvenel is an incisive critic of what he calls "primitivist nostalgia" (PT, 69), but he recognizes that this nostalgia is not merely the result of faulty doctrines or of irresponsible dreaming on the part of philosophers and revolutionaries. It has, in fact, deep and ineradicable roots in human nature. Human beings are made to live in face-to-face communities. The absence or weakening of communities of affection therefore necessarily gives rise to what Jouvenel calls "political infantilism"—"the mortal disease of advanced civilizations" (s, 160). Amid the perpetual change that characterizes modern society, human beings understandably long for the security and warmth of "the tribe." The desire for paternalistic government is a quasi-natural response to the inability of the anonymous Great Society to satisfy the natural human expectations for strong and intimate relations with our fellows. The appeal to collective solidarity and even uniformity is a misplaced application of the "natural ways" of the home to the national or worldwide community (PT, 69). The child, like the citizen of the closed community, comes to experience the benevolent attentions of "superior powers." Jouvenel suggestively remarks that the political "boss" who promises to provide for his underlings is in some ways a more natural embodiment of authority than the liberal magistrate who promises to pay "no regard to persons and 'merely follows the law'"(PT, 67).

In his discussion, Jouvenel dialectically oscillates between forceful denunciations of "political infantilism" and "primitivist nostalgia" on the one hand, and a subtle appreciation of the reasons for the continuing attraction of "the small closely-knit society" (s, 162) on the other. He understands that the small society still retains "an infinite attraction" for modern men. Even if it is strictly speaking unavailable as a political option, it retains some normative value as a reminder of the intrinsic good of the social tie itself.

For that reason, modern man must occasionally return to it in order "to renew his strength" (s, 162). Modern man "displays extraordinary vigor" when he reconnects with closely knit communities, whether in the form of the English public school or tight-knit revolutionary cells. But Jouvenel concludes that "any attempt to graft the same features on a large society is utopian and leads to tyranny" (s, 162). A careful and sympathetic student of Rousseau,[16] Jouvenel observes that the great French philosopher was wiser than many of his *soi-disant* disciples, such as Robespierre. This "pessimistic evolutionist" appreciated that large, populous, and developed states could never return to primitive simplicity. Rousseau's more modest aim was to check the progress of those societies that had not already committed themselves wholeheartedly to the adventure of modernity (s, 162n). Jouvenel appropriates Rousseau's critique of modern progress and puts it at the service of a chastened liberalism that accepts the inevitability of modern liberty but has no illusions that it is coextensive with moral progress.[17]

Jouvenel's unique brand of liberalism combines a profound appreciation of the benefits of modern civilization and the desirability of widespread individual initiatives with classical and

Rousseauan reservations about the moral effects of social progress. But he is careful to distinguish the necessary moral critique of modernity from the utopian urge to return to the world of the corollaries. Such a return, he repeatedly maintains, is both impossible and undesirable. In *Pure Theory*, Jouvenel introduces a concept that he calls "Galileo's law." This law states that "a structure, solid and serviceable at a given size, cannot stand if one seeks to reproduce it in a different order of size; that the much greater edifice has to be built on different lines" (PT, 69). The attempted return to primitive simplicity or classical harmony is thus destined to fail in its stated aim. Other means must be found to preserve civic affections in a modern society.

Jouvenel's objection to revolutionary or reactionary nostalgia for a lost communal treasure, though, is at bottom a moral one. The mutual affections that enrich human life cannot ultimately be imposed on society at large. Even a liberal political order, to be sure, needs civic affections and cannot ignore the question of the common good: Jouvenel is quite insistent on these points. But the effort to impose "intensive emotions" on the public life of a free society "is bound to wear thin." It is perfectly understandable that individuals who have difficulty finding meaningful human relations in their private lives will "dream of instituting" community at large. But Jouvenel warns that "love or friendship cannot be contrived by decree" (PT, 86). The spiritual dilemmas of modern societies cannot be overcome through political coercion or resort to a quasi-mythical legislator who aims to impose communal ties artificially. The forcible imposition of the dream of the harmonious city is bound "to generate hate more often than harmony"

(PT, 86). As the experience of communism amply attests, the real consequence of such efforts is to undermine the imperfect but real manifestations of community that continue to exist in liberal society. In such cases, the perfect truly is the enemy of the good.

Beyond Theoretical Modernity

Jouvenel is an incisive critic of communitarian illusions. But he is equally critical of the fundamental theoretical inadequacy of modern liberal political philosophy. This radical critique of modern theory is evident in each of his masterworks. He concluded *On Power* with an assault on "individualist rationalism," the "destructive metaphysic" that, in his view, made the development of totalitarianism a "certainty." Renewing Tocqueville's earlier account of the dialectical relationship between individualism and collectivism, Jouvenel attacks this metaphysic which sees in society nothing "but the state and the individual" (OP, 417). The proponents of individualist rationalism "disregarded the role of the spiritual authorities and of all those intermediate social forces which enframe, protect, and control the life of man, thereby obviating and preventing the intervention of Power." The partisans of individual liberation see in religion, the family, and a host of other intermediate institutions only the sources of despotism and as a result work to free human beings from dependence on any and all transpolitical authority. They do not appreciate that atheistic rationalism can give rise to new forms of cruelty and subservience and that human liberty depends on an acceptance of regulative principles beyond the power of the human will to alter. The "individualists and freethinkers" of the eighteenth and nineteenth centuries were committed to an abstract rationalism and a geometric account of social organization. They ignored the profound social utility and spiritual contribution of those "barriers and bulwarks" (OP, 417) under the ancien régime that acted as real restraints on the development of Power.

The weakening of spiritual authorities and intermediate social forces did not contribute, however, to a more humane society, as the partisans of Enlightenment rationalism had predicted. Instead, it undermined salutary restraints on "egotistical interests." Too many of the powerful and wealthy no longer acknowledged fundamental obligations to the poor or weak beyond those rooted in legal or contractual obligations. The weakening of religion and the gutting of traditional social restraints unleashed "blind passions leading to the fatal and inauspicious coming of tyranny" (OP, 417). The partisans of individualist liberalism did not appreciate that every society depends on a sense of noblesse oblige on the part of elites in positions of responsibility. In every community there are "rulers" and "guides" who set the tone for society at large (OP, 414). Even democracy cannot escape the inevitable division of society into the few and the many. The financier, the industrialist, the journalist, and the public relations agent must all be guided by a sense of obligation that "canalizes their activities toward social ends" (OP, 414).

But liberal society cherishes a "false dogma of equality" that is blind to the indispensable role of spiritual and social authorities within civil society. The "legalitarian" fiction that all social relations are merely contractual and that no individual or group has exceptional responsibilities both flatters the weak and "results in practice in a chartered libertinism for the strong" (OP, 414). In a liberal order, elites lack a defined sense of spiritual purpose. The liberal Jouvenel shares many of the reservations of both traditional conservatives and socialists about a merely "formal" conception of liberty. Liberalism only recognizes the political relevance of the individual and the state, and it has no place in its theory for the very authorities necessary to preserve a humane society.[18] Spiritual and social authorities have no formal political or legal status in a representative order and no officially acknowledged responsibilities. Liberals are torn between two equally problematic solutions to the spiritual vacuum brought about by egalitarian dogma: on the one hand, they succumb to spurious confidence in the ability of spontaneous order or an "invisible hand" to promote a common good rejected by liberalism's foundational premises; on the other hand, they come to support the dangerous statist imposition of social obligations through political command.

Jouvenel's analysis of the political consequences of individualist rationalism is by no means original to him. He acknowledges his debts on this score to a range of thinkers from Alexis de Tocqueville and August Comte to Hippolyte Taine. His particular contribution is to show that the rationalist metaphysic is not only destructive but false, rooted in the "willful" assumptions of early modern political philosophy. In *Sovereignty*, Jouvenel goes to great lengths to establish that a protoliberal thinker such as Hobbes fails to provide a principled basis for political liberty.[19] Hobbes fails to do so because he cannot account for the social nature of man or the nonarbitrary character of the moral life. But if self-restraint has no ultimate foundation in divine or natural law, then only the awesome restrictive powers of the state can keep egoism and blind passions at bay.

As we have seen, the development of civilization inevitably undermines the strong face-to-face ties that characterize traditional communal life. But it took a philosophic doctrine such as Hobbes's "fearful and atheistic individualism" to unleash hedonism and moral relativism as explicit principles of a political order. Jouvenel forthrightly rejects the Hobbesian notion that individual liberty can be understood "as the right of a man to obey his appetites," both because it ignores the higher capacities of the human soul and because it necessarily gives rise to the "strongest of powers," to "Leviathan," in order to "maintain society in being" (s, 298). Jouvenel insists that "the idea of political liberty is linked with other suppositions about man and with the encouragement of quite other tendencies" (s, 298). Hobbes's purported liberalism is based on an "arbitrary simplification" (s, 236) of the human world—one that cannot do justice to the manifold plurality of social life and the complexity of the human soul. Jouvenel indicates that contemporary liberals reject the political implications of Hobbes's individualism while accepting almost all of his reductionistic and relativistic premises. They fail to see that government based on free discussion and free opinion presupposes the human capacity to distinguish truth and falsehood and to define general principles of justice that transcend the human desire for power.

The Pure Theory of Politics contains one of Jouvenel's most powerful responses to the intellectual assumptions underlying modern liberalism. Part 2 of that work, "Setting: Ego in Otherdom," (PT, 57–87) is a rich articulation of the social nature of man. The larger purpose of *Pure Theory* is to analyze politics at the "micro level," to explore the foundation of politics in the capacity of "man to move man." This elementary exploration, however, does not presuppose any individualistic "methodological" assumptions. In order to avoid any misunderstandings on this score, Jouvenel devotes three chapters of *Pure Theory* to the exploration of ways that individuals exist in, and are profoundly shaped by, their social setting. He shows that the idea of what he calls Individual Man is, strictly speaking, an intellectual conceit that ignores the fundamental dependence of man on his wider social setting and a whole array of civilized inheritances. In this context, Jouvenel explicitly criticizes the "intellectual monstrosity" (PT, 60) that is social contract theory. He mocks the "fantasy of Individual Man striding about in Nature and deciding deliberately to come to terms with his fellows" (PT, 60). Jouvenel goes right for the jugular: social contract theories are the "views of childless men who must have forgotten their own childhood" (PT, 60). The "hardy, roving adults" of the state of nature could only imagine the advantages of the social state if they had already enjoyed the benefits of social existence in the family or some other protective setting.

Social contract theorists such as Hobbes ignore the "simple truth" that human beings "begin [their] lives as infants" (PT, 60). Therefore, when they enter civil social society human beings are never free of obligations to others. The first and indispensable society is the family, to which we owe our very existence and sense of humanity. The family provides a protective setting, a "humanized cosmos" (PT, 61), where the helpless child is loved and provided for. Human beings experience an exceptionally long period of de-

pendence on their begetters. But this extended period of dependence is a precondition for an education and moral training that
allow the young to begin to master complex individual and social
passions. The family and the extended social community provide
both group protection and group tuition (PT, 60)—they allow for
the education of the passions and inculcation in the ways of one's
people. The dependence of man on others therefore is a great—
indeed, the greatest—of blessings. Jouvenel argues that Hobbes's
claim that human beings construct an artificial political community out of the raw material of contentious and radically independent individuals is itself based on an unwarranted pride that forgets "that only dependence has made us what we are" (PT, 59).

The Wise Man as Debtor

Jouvenel's most eloquent discussion of human dependence can be
found in chapter 14 ("Liberty") of *Sovereignty*. In this chapter
Jouvenel argues that man's liberty and dignity depend on a gracious
acceptance of his status as a dependent being. Here the discussion
of human dependence goes beyond the family, which was the focus
in *Pure Theory*, to include an account of our debts and dependence
on tradition and the inheritances of civilization, the political
community that shapes our humanity, and the natural order itself.
Jouvenel defends natural piety against the false and acidic claims of
rational autonomy and individual independence. The battle cry of
eighteenth-century proponents of Enlightenment—"Man is born
free"—turns out to be the worst delusion. Jouvenel insists that it is
"the greatest nonsense if it is taken literally as a declaration of [the]

original and natural independence" (s, 316) of human beings. Human beings are in truth the product of "the prolonged efforts of others" within the family and the larger social order. Jouvenel echoes Burke's famous discussion of social contract theory in the *Reflections on the Revolution in France*. In that work Burke appropriated the language of contract theory to remind his contemporaries of its failure to do justice to the bonds connecting the living with those who came before them and those who will inherit their patrimony. Burke eloquently presents the true nature of the social contract:

> Society is indeed a contract. Subordinate contracts for objects of mere occasional interest may be dissolved at pleasure—but the state ought not to be considered as nothing better than a partnership agreement in a trade of pepper and coffee, callico or tobacco, or some other such low concern, to be taken up for a little temporary interest, and to be dissolved by the fancy of the parties. It is to be looked on with other reverence; because it is not a partnership in things subservient only to the gross animal existence of a temporary and perishable nature. It is a partnership in all science; a partnership in all art; a partnership in every virtue, and in all perfection. As the ends of such a partnership cannot be obtained in many generations, it becomes a partnership not only between those who are living, but between those who are living, those who are dead, and those who are to be born.[20]

Jouvenel renews this Burkean insight. He speaks of man as an "heir entering on the accumulated heritage of past generations, taking his place as a partner in a vastly wealthy association." He attacks the blindness of those who forget how "small and insignificant" (s, 317) Individual Man is, devoid as he is of this civilized inheritance.

Jouvenel aims to recover the sentiment of natural piety that is a precondition for man's recognition of his dependence on the Creator. "Every individual with a spark of imagination must feel deeply indebted to these many others, the living and the dead, the known and the unknown" (s, 317). Jouvenel emphasizes the naturalness of such piety and criticizes the "folly" of the modern emphasis on what society owes the individual. For Jouvenel, the fact of human dependence is much more than a natural datum. It is, more fully, a profoundly relevant moral truth. "The wise man knows himself for debtor, and his actions will be inspired by a deep sense of obligation" (s, 317). With this one sentence, he rejects the Promethean spirit common to all branches of modernity. In particular, Jouvenel sharply dissents from the classical liberal view of freedom and obligation put forward by John Stuart Mill at the beginning of *On Liberty*. There, Mill asserted that the individual ought to be free in those "parts of his life and conduct which affects only himself." For Jouvenel, there is something willful, narrow, even infantile about a view that ignores the obvious reality that "the whole of a man's life, whatever society he lives in, is passed in never-ending contact with his fellows; there is not a single action or even word of his which may not prove obnoxious, there is not one which is completely devoid of consequence for someone" (s, 315). Jouvenel believes that the individualist premises of Hobbes and Mill are not only destructive of a stable liberal order, but are based on a brutal contraction of the range of human obligations.

The libertarian premise of individual independence cannot provide a foundation for a sense of human dignity that does justice to the social nature of man.

Jouvenel believes that, if left unchecked, the individualist premises of modern liberalism will contribute to the subversion of liberty—that individualism contains a collectivist logic that can eventuate in tyranny, or at least in the serious erosion of the social fabric. The soullessness of "Babylon," the modern atheistic state that officially acknowledges no principle above the individual and collective will, is psychologically untenable: human beings are made for community. The undermining of social friendship and vigorous intermediate social groupings are too much for many fine souls to bear. In particular, the contemporary intellectual's disdain for the impersonality of the modern state and society gives rise to an understandable but finally tyrannical desire to re-create community as an imagined "Icaria," freed from the emptiness of life in Babylon. But Icaria is always located too close to the sun.

Babylon and Icaria

Babylon is Jouvenel's name for a "large and complex social whole, far advanced in civilization" (all quotations in this section from s, 328–33). His account of the intellectual and political development of Babylon is, in truth, a reasonably accurate sketch of the profound transformations within the liberal West over the past three or four centuries. Babylon is a commercial society marked by "every sort of activity and a wide variety of ways of life." Religious orthodoxy, if not religion itself, "has been in decline there for some time," and philosophers have successfully challenged "old metaphysical and moral certitudes." Efforts at crafting a rational system of morals as an alternative to those grounded in revealed religion have failed. As a result, Babylonians face "a long-drawn-out intellectual crisis." Babylonians confront a great diversity of ways of life, but, even more importantly, a dizzying array of beliefs and opinions. Babylonians cannot agree on "what is seemly, what is moral, what is just, what is owing." In contrast to Rousseau, however, Jouvenel acknowledges that Babylonian society continues to function more or less satisfactorily. Babylonian laws do not reflect a shared moral understanding or any kind of agreement about what is good in itself. Babylon is held together by a "system of laws of pragmatic inspiration, which forbids action of a kind harmful to the social organism and commands behavior necessary to social prosperity." The liberal or Babylonian state is strictly speaking "neutral and agnostic" when it comes to claims about the human good, to cite Pierre Manent's striking formulation.[21] It respects the diversity of activities and opinions that proliferate in a free society. It does not appeal to a common system of beliefs in order to elicit obedience from free men. But behind the liberal state lurks the Hobbesian specter of "fear of punishments induced by a strong government." The principles of governance in modern societies are essentially Hobbesian.

The prosperous, law-bound, commercial society therefore may be the "freest" in the history of the world, but to some sensitive souls it appears to impose insufferable burdens that stifle individual conscience and human spontaneity. Its freedom depends on an "apparatus of repression," its laws ignore the naturally obligatory character of conscience. The spiritually disenchanted long for a society without law or repression, one where obligations are voluntarily fulfilled, where conscience replaces an arbitrary system of command. They are attracted to revolutionary movements that promise to "reconstitute a small, primitive society in the heart of the large, highly civilized society." These revolutionary sectarians experience "the unity of principles and the spontaneous harmony of behaviors." They yearn to "bend the rest of the Babylonians to a system of rules which is coherent, rational and complete." But Babylonians do not welcome revolution as liberation. They experience the "march to total liberty" as the fanatical imposition of restraints by a revolutionary sect that does not share the views of Babylonians at large. There is nothing spontaneous or conscientious about the attempted revolutionary transformation of society.

Babylonians thus understandably yearn for the freedoms of the old Hobbesian order and are repelled by the moral fanaticism that animates the revolutionary impulse. Jouvenel's account is undoubtedly incomplete as a description of the development of totalitarianism or even of the psychology of conspiratorial, tyrannical sects. But it incisively highlights the specific vulnerability of the liberal order: the "neutral and agnostic" state is experienced as profoundly unnatural by those who are sensitive to the connection between conscience and law, by those who "think of laws as the expression of a moral rule." And despite the "official" claims of liberalism, it is impossible for human beings to wholly sever the natural connection between law and morality.

The experience of totalitarianism in the twentieth century has gone a long way toward discrediting revolutionary politics in the Western world, at least for the foreseeable future. Jouvenel suggests, however, that the dialectic of Babylon and Icaria is inherent in the modern adventure. "The dream of Icaria is forever being born again spontaneously in the heart of Babylon. For men never resign themselves to Babylon being Babylon." As much as we rightly loathe totalitarianism, we ought to welcome this stubborn refusal of human beings to resign themselves to spiritual desiccation. It is profoundly natural for human beings to pose the question of the common good. Even in liberal societies, in the "procedural republic" that is Babylon, human beings long for those "islands of friendship" that reveal to them that they are social beings dependent on others for almost everything they are. Therefore the inevitably totalitarian character of the Icarian revolution should not discredit the necessary effort to free the common good from the prison of the corollaries.

Conclusion

We have seen that Jouvenel's thought is characterized by an unresolved tension between a progressive confidence in the open or dynamic society and profoundly classical reservations about the moral consequences of modernity. Jouvenel sides with modern liberty against the closed city or primitive community while also drawing on the broad tradition of classical and Christian thought to expose the intrinsic limitations of modern political philosophy. Jouvenel's measured ambivalence about things ancient and modern, and his dialectical appropriation and critique of aspects of modern theory and practice, reflect his desire to do justice to the complexity of the human world. By posing the question of the common good within the context of the modern liberal order, Jouvenel reveals the fatal limitations of the liberal reduction of social reality to the sole realities of the state and the individual, as well as the deluded character of all forms of "primitivist nostalgia." Jouvenel thereby encourages each of us to do justice to the various goods of life, including the inherent diversity of human nature, the humanizing requirements of conscience, and the social bonds that make both true individuality and community possible.

CHAPTER FOUR

THE SPIRIT OF SOVEREIGNTY AND THE REGULATED WILL

THE IDEA THAT ALL POLITICAL legitimacy derives from the "sovereign" people seems as natural to modern man as the morning sun. The formulations of this idea vary but their common intent is clear: both leaders and citizens of modern democracies speak effortlessly about the sovereign people, "the consent of the governed" and "the general will." "The sovereignty of the people" moreover was affirmed by all of the contenders in the great ideological drama of the twentieth century—even Communist and Nazi totalitarians claimed to adequately represent the will of the people or the nation. Modern politics as a whole is marked less fundamentally by a rejection of the idea of absolute rule than by an insistence that all rule must ultimately emanate from the people. To be sure, liberal or constitutional democracies make every effort to balance the claims of individual and collective sovereignty. In accord with the wisdom of Montesquieu, they have established complex institutional mechanisms to ensure that "power checks power." It has even been argued that liberal democracy remains a moderate form of government precisely because it promotes a "neutralization" of sovereignty that to a considerable degree masks and effectively curtails the "willful" nature of all human claims to sovereignty.[1]

In modern times, the idea of sovereignty provided Power with a crucial weapon for subduing the temporal authority of the church. First the emperor, then the monarch acting as "emperor in his kingdom," then the people acting in the name of the general will, claimed for themselves the "plentitude of power" that had earlier been attributed to the Roman pontiff as God's true representative on earth (s, 207–8). If theocracy was a corruption of the biblical imperative to "obey God rather than men"(Acts 5:29)—that is, if the Catholic Church recognized in principle "things that are Caesar's" (Matthew 22:20–22)—absolute sovereignty, what Jouvenel calls "sovereignty in itself"(s, 234–37), seems to be intrinsic to the very project of philosophical modernity. True friends of human liberty are confronted with a disconcerting dilemma: there are grave dangers associated both with affirming and rejecting an order of things above the human will. Is it possible to oppose the totalitarianism implicit in all merely human claims to sovereignty without returning to religious authoritarianism and without spurning the considerable achievements of liberal constitutionalism? The modern solution to the problem of clerical authoritarianism has engendered forms of secular religion that pose an even greater threat to human integrity than the "pious cruelty" so fiercely denounced by the early modern political philosophers.[2] How is it possible, then, to avoid an unnatural despotism of the spirit over the body, of the church over the city, without compromising the spiritual foundations of human liberty?

The writings of Bertrand de Jouvenel provide a particularly helpful and largely untapped resource for overcoming this impasse. Rejecting the fundamental premise of philosophical modernity, the fallacious belief that man is an "autonomous" being who "constructs" himself and his world, Jouvenel limns a conception of political liberty that rejects all claims to human sovereignty. Because no human being is sovereign over himself, he has no right to exercise absolute and arbitrary rule over other human beings. In a most politic manner, the French political philosopher brings together Christian constitutionalism and the best of the modern liberal heritage. He provides a philosophical grounding for the reconciliation of "the spirit of religion" and "the spirit of freedom" that Tocqueville believed was the great challenge facing friends of liberty in a democratic age.[3]

We have already suggested that the constitutional checks and balances associated with liberal constitutionalism serve to mask the theoretical radicalism at the heart of philosophical modernity. Despite their manifold differences, all the major philosophical currents of modernity affirm what the Hungarian moral and political philosopher Aurel Kolnai has called the "self-sovereignty" of man, the idea that man is finally sovereign master over himself.[4] Bertrand de Jouvenel was one of a very small group of political philosophers in the twentieth century who truly appreciated the audacious radicalism of the modern philosophical project. He rejected any conception of liberty that denied permanent principles above the human will that limit and inform the human exercise of freedom. He was a partisan instead of the "regulated will" (s, 247–49) and an incisive critic of "sovereignty in itself," the triumph of human willfulness that he associated with such modern thinkers as Hobbes and Descartes.

In Jouvenel's view, Hobbes's *Leviathan* gave perfect expression to this new spirit of unchecked human mastery. In order to put an end to Europe's theological-political problem, Hobbes posited an "arbitrary simplification" (s, 236) of reality, a simplification that had immense practical consequences for the subsequent development of the Western world. Hobbes openly denied the existence of any principles of right and wrong antecedent to the formation of the social contract. His "fearful and atheistic individualism" (s, 236) ignored the natural complexity of the social order, denied the existence of any superintending moral principles above the human will, and reduced social reality to the "single pair" (s, 237) of the individual and the state. Beginning with the most radically individualistic and hedonistic premises, Hobbes articulated a thoroughly secular foundation for absolute political sovereignty. It might even be said that he invented sovereignty, at least in its distinctively modern form. In *Leviathan*, man was reconceived as "the maker and matter" of the human world.[5] Modern totalitarianism is unthinkable without this premise, even if Hobbes's political intent was ultimately more liberal than despotic. Locke, Pufendorf, Rousseau and a host of other modern thinkers would try to constrain Hobbesian "absolutism" without challenging his assumption of the self-sovereignty of man, the essential pillar of the entire edifice. Their "starting point," wrote Jouvenel, "is Hobbes: they think in terms of Hobbes" (s, 237). In contrast, Jouvenel affirms the "givenness" of reality and attacks the political "Protagorism," as he calls it, at the heart of modernity, the demonic conceit that "man is the measure of all things" (OP, 234). The effort to construct a self-sufficient human order that rejects the authority of God, the natural law, and the practical wisdom inherent in customary law had given rise to what Jouvenel calls "the rationalist crisis" (OP, 231–34). In response to this crisis, Jouvenel insists that there must be a return to an older wisdom—that of Aristotle, St. Thomas, and Montesquieu—that combines prudence and natural law in a manner that still speaks to the concerns of modern man (OP, 350). Jouvenel's analysis of "the rationalist crisis" and his critique of "sovereignty in itself" are grounded in an affirmation of the natural order of things and united to a thoroughgoing rejection of moral relativism and social constructivism in all their forms.

In a measured tone and through the medium of political philosophy, Jouvenel renews the traditional Catholic critique of modernity's effort to emancipate the human will. But, crucially, Jouvenel appropriates and employs that critique at the service of moderate and humane politics. In his judgment, human liberty can only be sustained if there is deference to something permanent above the human will. The modern critique of a "higher law" and a "natural order of things" began as an understandable effort to defend the autonomy of politics against the intrusions of clerical authoritarianism (S, 218). The proponents of the secular state understandably wished to overcome the religious strife that was so destructive of civic peace and social stability. By emancipating the will, however, they paved the way for intellectual currents and political movements that subverted the very meaning of law and promoted the full-scale totalitarian manipulation of human beings. In the end, the assumptions of philosophical modernity cannot sus-

tain the constitutional liberties that are rightly the glory of Western man.

Jouvenel certainly appreciated that the emancipation of the
human will could not have occurred without the insuperable difficulty that the Christian church posed for the autonomy of the
European political order. He does not, however, bring the theological-political problem to the foreground of his analysis. He discusses it intelligently and shows every awareness of the arbitrariness of the modern solution to it, but he does not sufficiently emphasize the fact that modernity's arbitrary simplification of reality
was put forward as a solution to a vexing problem that traditional
political science and moral philosophy seemed powerless to address. It may have been an inadequate solution but it was a solution nonetheless. On this score, the work of the contemporary
French political philosopher Pierre Manent provides a helpful
complement to Jouvenel's reflection. Like Jouvenel, Manent highlights the modern "emancipation of the will" and attempts to show
that no satisfactory political arrangements can be grounded solely
on the principle of the human will.[6] Yet his work goes further than
Jouvenel's in detailing and emphasizing the problem that gave rise
to the fantastic project of human self-sovereignty in the first place.[7]
He helps make the Hobbesian simplification of reality seem a little
less arbitrary, if no less inadequate. Consider Manent's remarkable
1993 essay "Christianity and Democracy."[8] In addition to showing
how philosophical modernity originated as a response to the intractability of the European theological-political problem, Manent's
essay provides an invaluable account of the traditional Catholic
critique of modernity. His discussion illuminates the ways in which

the Catholic rejection of philosophical modernity and the liberal critique of totalitarian democracy share a common rejection of the unfettered human will. Manent's essay helps clarify Jouvenel's effort to reconcile Christianity and liberalism without pretending that the historic opposition between these two great antagonists was nothing more than an unfortunate misunderstanding.

The Catholic Critique of the Sovereign Will

Today it is all too easy to dismiss the longstanding Catholic critique of modernity as evidence of the church's lamentable refusal to come to terms with intellectual, scientific, and moral progress. As Leo Strauss observed in his seminal essay "Progress or Return?" for the modern intellectual the distinction between what is "progressive" and "reactionary" has largely superseded the age-old distinction between right and wrong, good and evil.[9] For those imbued with the spirit of "progress," to oppose the dominant currents of the age is to be nothing short of intellectually perverse and morally obtuse. Such progressivism or historicism is by no means confined to secular intellectual quarters. Many Catholic thinkers today are embarrassed by what they see as the pre–Vatican II church's obdurate opposition to the modern project. They welcome what they see as the church's recent embrace not only of political democracy but also of many of the most questionable assumptions of modern thought. Instead of pursuing a prudential accommodation of the church to the realities of the age, they "kneel before the world" and judge the old Christian wisdom by the criteria of modernity, rather than the other way around.[10] The writings of

Jouvenel and Manent both point in another and much more promising direction. Instead of choosing between indiscriminate opposition to modernity or an equally foolhardy genuflection before the altar of progress, they subject the church's traditional opposition to the project of human sovereignty to the bar of human reason, to the clarifying light of political philosophy. In doing so, they establish that the church's opposition to modernity was much more than misguided resistance to progress. Despite errors of judgment and tone, the church had a much deeper grasp of the logic and consequences of modernity than the vast majority of modernity's critics or supporters.

In "Christianity and Democracy" Pierre Manent argues that the church initially could not accept the legitimacy of the secular state precisely because it believed it to be an essentially atheistic enterprise, the political manifestation of a philosophical project to free man from obedience to the authority of God. In light of the aggressive rationalism of the continental Enlightenment and the militant anti-Christian spirit of the French Revolution, the church judged that "the primary purpose" of the liberal state was "to institutionalize the sovereignty of the human will."[11] The church did not share the benign assumption, dear to more recent scholarship, that the secular state was a merely practical or technical solution to a political problem that entailed no subversive metaphysical assumptions about the nature of man and the world. The church saw more deeply. From the French Revolution until Pope Pius X's condemnation of "modernism" in the 1907 encyclical *Pascendi*, "the Church judged in its wisdom . . . that the modern political and intellectual movement *willed* the eradication of the true religion."[12]

It is particularly tempting for Americans to dismiss this as the over-wrought judgment of a reactionary papacy, an understandable if intemperate response to the extremism of the continental Enlight-enment. America, it is often suggested, reveals the possibility of a different, more moderate Enlightenment, one that allows believers of different stripes to live together in peace without intending to eradicate religion or deny the transcendent authority of God. The American example does show that liberalism need not be explicitly motivated by aggressive hostility to revealed religion. As Michael Novak has demonstrated in *On Two Wings*, many of the founders were believing Christians, and almost all of them appreciated the importance of religion to the moral health of a self-governing re-public.[13] But these considerations do not exhaust the matter. Even or especially in America, "the dogma of the sovereignty of the people" is the alpha and the omega of the political world.[14] Tocqueville saw with great perspicuity that that dogma's fundamen-tal tenet, the principle of consent, would come to transform "the majority of human actions."[15] No authority, whether the church, family, or university, would in the long term be immune from the revolutionary effects of the doctrine of consent. That is, even the most moderate democracy partakes of modernity's revolutionary intent and logic. Americans may not speak the incendiary language of the general will, but they wittingly or unwittingly accept its core presuppositions. The question of the relative moderation or im-moderation of democratic sovereignty, then, cannot be settled by pious invocations of the "original intent" of the founders or by his-torical studies showing that practical men did not always fully ap-preciate what was entailed in the affirmation of political sovereignty.

For its part, the Roman church believed that the "spirit of sovereignty" was essentially atheistic.[16] But as Manent judiciously suggests, it is necessary to distinguish between an "atheism of presupposition and implication" and an "atheism of affirmation."[17] Even the most lawful and moderate versions of liberalism enshrined human autonomy and mocked "monkish superstition." The church in its wisdom knew that man cannot serve both God and self: to "affirm this 'autonomy' or 'sovereignty' is to deny," at least implicitly, "the existence of God."[18] The forceful lucidity of the church's opposition to modern sovereignty therefore was its greatest strength, but also a considerable vulnerability. How could the church tutor the liberal movement, as it eventually sought to do, when it thunderously condemned modernity root and branch? And was such a categorical condemnation of modernity and all its works finally compatible with the prudence that the church traditionally recognized as the first of the political virtues?

Of course, some Catholic voices persisted in refusing any accommodation with the "modern world" and continued to identify liberalism in all its forms with a demonic revolt against God. They yearned for a restoration of the lost unity of Christendom and hoped that modernity would somehow pass like a bad dream. In contrast, modern popes such as Leo XIII and Pius XII adopted a more statesmanlike perspective. They encouraged a prudential reconciliation between Christianity and more moderate forms of constitutional liberalism without in any way abandoning the church's traditional opposition to the project of human sovereignty. They took solace in the fact that saner liberals had largely made their peace with God and the natural order of things. As Manent suggestively remarks, since God was stronger than the "satanic pride of the Enlightenment," some "restoration" of good sense (if not Christendom) was clearly inevitable. The church, "which has concern for men," could not continue to simply "curse" liberal or bourgeois society.[19]

The church was not wrong to identify modern liberalism with the sovereignty of the human will, with the audacious effort to "institutionalize the sovereignty of the human will, to substitute the latter for the law of God or for the finalities, aptitudes, and necessities of the nature of man."[20] For such was surely the self-conscious intent of such architects of modernity as Machiavelli and Hobbes. In addition, the concept of the will is the connecting thread running through all the currents of philosophical modernity from Machiavelli to Nietzsche via Rousseau, Kant, and Hegel.[21] Today, however, as we confront the prosaic realities of contemporary democratic life, we have difficulty comprehending "the extraordinary audacity of the original project of establishing the human world on the narrow point of the human will."[22] It is easy to forget the radical assumptions underlying such commonplace ideas as consent and popular sovereignty. We are confronted with a paradox: our democracies both embody and subvert the natural order of things. But in light of a totalitarianism which took up the spirit of sovereignty with a truly demonic intensity, both Christians and liberals rallied to the defense of the "real" world of family, property, religion, and liberty against the revolutionary effort to establish utopia-in-power. As Alain Besançon has shown, both the church and liberals found themselves allied in the common defense of civilization against the ideological deformation of reality.[23] In the middle of the twentieth century, antitotalitarian statesmen such as Churchill and de Gaulle spoke freely of the need to preserve "liberal and Christian civilization" against the totalitarian threat.[24] This antiutopian or antitotalitarian reconciliation of Christians and liberals was prefigured by the turn taken by French liberalism after the French Revolution. Thinkers such as Constant, Royer-Collard, Guizot, and Tocqueville, whatever their other differences, were united by a common revulsion at the effects of unlimited sovereignty. They recoiled at the terror and tyranny imposed in the name of the sovereign people. They came to recognize, in Constant's famous words, that "there are some weights too heavy for the hands of men."[25] These liberals found themselves joining forces with Christians to oppose the self-assertion of the human will. In doing so, they invited Christians to rally to a chastened liberalism that had learned what the church in some sense knew all along. Manent's essay powerfully evokes this remarkable turn of events. In light of French revolutionary nihilism, in response to the fury of the unleashed human will, liberals rediscovered the salutary role of religion. As a result, religion found "its specifically modern political and moral credibility."[26] What had once been the defect of religion became its indispensable merit: "it is something above the human will."[27] If liberals did not exactly reaffirm the sovereignty of God, they rejected the political consequences of the sovereignty of man. If they could not proclaim the sovereignty of God as a formal political principle without reverting to a clerical or confessional state, they freely acknowledged that the self-deification of man led to the worst forms of totalitarian bondage.

Jouvenel, a Catholic and lover of human liberty, drew freely from these previous discussions. In part 3 of *Sovereignty*, titled "The Sovereign" (s, 201–57), Jouvenel examines the modern idea of sovereignty as an effort to free man from any superintending authority above the human will. In the three chapters of this section of his book, Jouvenel judiciously draws upon traditional Catholic and (conservative) liberal critiques of modern "willfulness." He not only sketches a forceful and persuasive critique of "sovereignty in itself" but shows that the emancipated will is incompatible with the moral presuppositions of democratic self-government. In his thorough dissection of the claims of absolute sovereignty, Jouvenel draws upon the insights of both the jurists of the French "old regime" (the so-called parliamentarians) and the postrevolutionary French liberals in order to sketch a compelling account of what he calls the "regulated will" (s, 247–49), which he argues is the true foundation of human and political liberty. He maintains that the freedom and dignity of man depend on recognition of the sovereignty of God and the moral authority of the natural law. But as a political liberal he does not want the sovereignty of God to become a direct principle of political life. That is the path of theocracy, a path that was never the considered choice of the Christian West. Jouvenel understands that free political life owes more to the prudence of decent men than to misplaced efforts to divine God's intent amidst the changing currents of human affairs. Jouvenel appeals instead to a "higher law" that has an indirect effect on politics but is no less crucial for that. This higher law serves to relativize every human claim to absolute rule over the bodies and souls of men. Jouvenel's distinctive reconciliation of Catholicism and liberalism stands out because of his insistence that true liberalism must self-consciously reject the founding premises of modern sovereignty. He calls for something much more daring than a merely pragmatic or tactical reconciliation between the two old and exhausted contestants in Europe's centuries-old theological-political dispute.

The Two Old Regimes: From the Ladder of Commands to Absolutism

In chapter 10 of *Sovereignty* ("On the Idea of the Sovereign Will"), Jouvenel provides a suggestive outline of "the extraordinary progress and emancipation of the Sovereign Will in the course of European history" (s, 202). He contrasts the modern idea of sovereignty with the limited conception of political power that prevailed throughout the Middle Ages. His account of the development of sovereignty is a supplement to *On Power*'s earlier description of the rise of the modern collectivist state —he notes with some foreboding that "the growth of the idea of Sovereignty" is coextensive with "the growth of Power" in modern times (s, 201). In these pages, Jouvenel presents in broad strokes the story of the transition from the European old regime to recognizably modern politics, a transition mediated by that perplexing halfway house called "absolutism." The absolutist monarchies of Europe shattered the customary arrangements of the traditional European "constitution" without completely jettisoning the Christian heritage of the West. As Pierre Manent has so well described, the idea of a momentous transition from an old order to a new one was shared by a wide array of nineteenth-century thinkers (e.g., Guizot, Comte, Tocqueville, and Marx) who were writing at or near the end of this process.

These thinkers all believed that Europeans had lived through an immense historical transformation. This overwhelming sense of having witnessed a great, inexorable historical mutation contributed mightily to the modern conviction that "History" (with a capital *H*) rather than "nature" was the fundamental category of human and political existence.[28] Part 3 of *Sovereignty* provides an extraordinary account of this transition from the old to the new order, but it does so without succumbing to the historicist premise that modern man has no access to an order of things that transcends the distinction between the old and new dispensations.

Hans Morgenthau saw in Jouvenel's writings a "reactionary" nostalgia for the Middle Ages, for an age when power was limited and the idea of absolute sovereignty was repugnant to self-respecting men.[29] There is no doubt that Jouvenel admired the medieval rejection of human voluntarism and unlimited state power. In that respect, at least, he believed that our medieval forebears understood truths that we moderns have a difficult time comprehending. But, as we argued in chapter 2, Jouvenel expressed no nostalgia for an era where inequalities were rampant and where there was precious little room for personal initiative or technological innovation. Instead, Jouvenel wished to promote a conception of moral limits and political restraint that is appropriate to a dynamic, modern civilization. In his view, historical studies are valuable not because they provide a road map for returning to a mythical golden age but because they allow us to see how theoretical mistakes can be rectified within the modern world that we are destined to inhabit.

Let us turn now to the medieval order, to that moment in Western political consciousness when absolute sovereignty was still unrecognizable (s, 202–3). Contrary to a widespread misconception, Jouvenel shows that the Middle Ages knew no such idea as "the divine right of kings." That was a later innovation put forward by apologists for "absolutist" Stuart and Bourbon monarchies in both Britain and France (s, 202, 238). Medieval man, in contrast, rejected every conception of absolute sovereignty. "In the Middle Ages men had a very strong sense of that concrete thing, hierarchy; they lacked the idea of that abstract thing, sovereignty" (s, 203). In the Middle Ages, to be sure, every man had to pay his dues to his superiors within the "great chain of duties" (s, 204). He had clearly demarcated responsibilities to those above him in the order of command. Every man had a superior, a sire, seignor, or sovereign, and that superior also had his superior in the "ladder of commands" (s, 204). Jouvenel describes an intricate network in which command was never absolute but always circumscribed by the rights and claims of the different actors within the inherently plural hierarchy of medieval life. The medieval order entailed a "tiered system of rights" (s, 206) in which the king served as the final arbiter but never as the ultimate source of law or legitimacy. Whatever its other limitations, medieval Europe was an essentially libertarian civilization. Medieval Christians rejected the Roman imperial idea of a "single master monopolizing all authority and enjoying the plentitude of power" (s, 206). At the same time, if the imperial idea went into abeyance, it was by no means interred. As we have seen, the idea of "the plentitude of power" was resurrected by the jurists and canonists of the Church of Rome who wanted to affirm its sovereign authority over the spiritual and (if only indirectly) temporal realms. In reaction to the absolutist claims made on behalf of the church, advocates of the autonomy of the secular realm such as Dante and Marsilius of Padua put forth absolutist claims of their own on behalf of the empire and secular political authority (s, 206, 218). This pattern would be reprised in another key in the early modern period, when political philosophers defended the sovereignty of man against claims made on behalf of the sovereignty of God. Jouvenel's historical analysis provides ample support for Pierre Manent's argument that the Christian church posed a "structural" problem for the integrity and autonomy of the civil authority.[30] As a result, the modern defenders of an autonomous temporal realm found no way to affirm the independence of the political realm without also asserting a dangerous absolutism and without denying an order of things above the human will (s, 218) to which it should conform.

It was the kings of France and Britain who first succeeded in establishing an "absolute" secular power that rivaled the claims of papal authority. Taking their bearings from the papal assertion of the "plentitude of power" for the church, they aimed for a monopolization of power within their own realms. This served to establish the state's independence vis-à-vis the church while breaking the monarchy's dependence on the various petty sovereigns within the ladder of medieval command (s, 212–14). No longer would kings be so dependent on the good will or financial generosity of nobles and burghers. From the fourteenth to the end of the sixteenth and the beginning of the seventeenth centuries, Europeans witnessed a gradual displacement of the first old regime, with its "graded superiorities" (s, 215), by a new old regime where kings assumed a monopoly of supreme power. But Jouvenel demonstrates

that emergent absolutism entailed something far less than the assertion of "willful" human authority. As the great French jurist
Charles L'Oyseau wrote in 1608, the absolute rule of kings was still
limited by the sovereignty of God, the authority of the natural law,
and "the fundamental laws of the state" (s, 220). In *Sovereignty*,
Jouvenel provides a detailed examination of L'Oyseau's writings
precisely because they reveal the simultaneous radicalism and moderation of European absolutism, the uneasy and finally incoherent
compromise between human self-assertion and deference to traditional moral and customary authority.

The Ambiguities of Absolutism

L'Oyseau was a contemporary of Henri IV and published his *Traité
des seigneuries* (1608) near the end of the transition period from
medieval to absolutist conceptions of sovereignty. His work has the
merit of making clear the essential ambiguity of absolutism, torn as
it was between moderation and the assertion of the "unlimited
power and authority" (s, 217) of the state. In the manner of
traditional jurists and political thinkers, L'Oyseau carefully distinguished "the different species of superiority." As Jouvenel writes, he
"meticulously distinguishes ownership (*sieurerie*), seignory, suzer-
ainty, sovereignty." Furthermore, he posited a fundamental distinction between private and public seignory and privileged the
sovereignty of the royal authority over the "superiority" exercised
by the nobility (s, 214–15). According to L'Oyseau, private seignory
principally concerns the individual's right over his property, while
the public sovereign exercises supreme command over the state and

society as a whole. In marked contrast to the medieval conception of a ladder of plural and limited authorities, L'Oyseau conceived the state as "the summit of authority," which "knows no limits" (s, 215, 218). The political landscape he described was already recognizably modern: the "whole force of rights have been concentrated in the two extremities," the individual and the state (s, 216). If there were limits inherent in sovereign power there would be a need for a superior authority that could enforce such limits. L'Oyseau believed that such limits would undermine the "perfection" of the public power. Jouvenel convincingly observes that L'Oyseau was too concerned with the abstract "perfection" of sovereign authority and insufficiently appreciative of the concrete relations that characterize nondespotic political life. But L'Oyseau's abstract preference for absolutism did not lead him to support arbitrariness in politics or to reject the authority of the moral law. To begin with, the sovereign state was in his view obliged to protect the full range of private liberties, particularly the right to property. For L'Oyseau, liberty and property were "conceived as antecedent . . . to the public authority" and therefore characterized by an "absolutely independent existence" (s, 219). L'Oyseau, then, was committed both to a logic that asserted the perfection of the public power and to a recognition of rights and duties antecedent to the human will and thus immune in principle to public manipulation. This "traditional" deference to a higher law, to the requirements of religion, and to rights of property, served in Jouvenel's view the salutary purpose of "weaken[ing] the absoluteness of sovereignty" (s, 219).

Jouvenel's detailed account of L'Oyseau's complex conception of sovereignty is quite instructive. It cogently shows that absolut-

ism was an unstable halfway house between traditional conceptions of legitimacy and authority and the modern ambition to build
a political world solely on the principle of the human will. By the
beginning of the seventeenth century, sovereignty had already become "a prodigiously healthy plant" (s, 221). The old moral constitution of Europe was, however, far from moribund. It still com-
manded the attention and respect of many thoughtful European
jurists and statesmen, not least of all L'Oyseau himself. But with
the later Enlightenment's radical assault on traditional philosophy
and religion, with the rise of "irreligion, legal positivism and the
sovereignty of the people" (s, 221) as reigning dogmas among intellectual elites, modern sovereignty was able to resume "its indefinite
growth" (s, 221). The theoreticians of absolutist monarchy were
not yet ready to deny the sovereignty of God or the superintending
authority of the natural law. But for all intents and purposes, they
had ceded intellectual momentum to the more consistent and "willful" proponents of absolute sovereignty. Why stop at the authority
of kings when you can affirm the sovereign authority of the people,
nay, of the entire human race? Why rest content with a halfway
house like Christian absolutism when "sovereignty in itself" has
been painted in the most alluring colors by the greatest thinkers of
the age?

What, then, is Jouvenel's considered judgment on the second,
absolutist old regime? How does one make sense of the mixture of
restraint and ambition, tradition and modernity, that marked the
absolutist transition to modern democracy? There are no simple
answers to these questions. At times, Jouvenel praises absolutist
Europe for its refusal to jettison the European moral heritage. At

other moments, he attacks an absolutist king such as Louis XIV as nothing more than a despotic precursor of the Jacobins and Napoleon (s, 222). The Sun King destroyed precious traditions, liberties, prerogatives, and privileges even if he exercised his power with considerably more restraint than the revolutionary tyrants of later centuries (s, 222). In the same chapter, Jouvenel writes in a Burkean spirit about the undeniable continuities that still existed between the moral assumptions of absolutist France and the precious inheritance of medieval and Christian Europe. In crucial respects, absolutist Europe still belonged to the world before human sovereignty, a world that had not yet subordinated justice to the demands of the human will. At the same time, Jouvenel agrees with Tocqueville's famous thesis in *The Old Regime and the Revolution* that the centralizing propensities of absolutist monarchy were an indispensable stage in the development of the modern collectivist state. He also shares Tocqueville's repugnance for the *beamtenstaat*—the bureaucratic state—and likewise loathes the moral and political consequences of absolute sovereignty in all its forms. He therefore freely mocks the partisans of popular sovereignty who were unaware that they were continuing the work of the Stuarts and Bourbons of old (s, 238).

In the end, however, Jouvenel's target was less absolutism as a political doctrine or regime than the terrible "emancipation of the will" that absolutism both spawned and checked. Jouvenel's real target is what he calls "sovereignty in itself." Unlike defenders of absolutism such as Bossuet and L'Oyseau, who denounced arbitrariness and defended the sovereignty of reason and justice (s, 251–52), the advocates of pure sovereignty were philosophers who decisively broke with the premodern religious and philosophical inheritance of the West. In their different ways, Descartes and Hobbes rejected both customary authority and the natural law and posited the autonomous individual as the starting point for moral and philosophical reflection. In their universe, "all begins with the individual, all comes back to him" (s, 236). In their universe, natural right is nothing more than the individual power of each and justice is essentially a contrivance to satisfy human needs. Hobbes's absolute sovereign serves the needs of individuals; he is more bourgeois and "liberal" than tyrannical, as we have already observed. But such sovereign power is inherently dangerous because it rests on no other authority than the human will and respects no intrinsic limits or sacred restraints. This audacious conception of sovereignty is the common foundation, the shared patrimony, of both liberal democratic and totalitarian modernity. "Sovereignty in itself" is, in Jouvenel's view, the enemy of true constitutionalism, a constitutionalism that needs to rest on much sturdier foundations if it is to do its work and last. In chapter 12 of *Sovereignty*, Jouvenel sketches his alternative to conceptions of democratic sovereignty that depend on the presuppositions of philosophical modernity. He calls this alternative "the regulated will" and makes clear that it entails a complete rejection of the modernist transvaluation of will and justice (s, 231–33). Let us now turn to that important discussion.

The Regulated Will

"Man is no great inventor of ideas," Jouvenel remarks at the beginning of *Sovereignty*'s twelfth chapter ("The Theory of the

Regulated Will and 'Fortunate Powerlessness'"). The same political and philosophical mistakes keep reappearing with depressing
regularity, even as their partisans reassure themselves about the
revolutionary character of their ideas. This is particularly the case
with proponents of "the sovereignty of the people," who exaggerate
the originality of their insights as well as the extent of their
departure from the politics of the past. In the tradition of Constant,
Guizot, and Tocqueville, Jouvenel aimed to discredit those theories
of popular sovereignty which claim that the will of the sovereign
people is the true source of law and legitimacy. He rejects as false
and impious the idea that the people are free to will anything for
themselves since they are the only source of legitimate command.
In his view, the champions of the unbridled popular sovereignty at
the heart of the French Revolution dressed the old absolutism in
new clothes while thoughtlessly discarding the implicit awareness
of limits that still restrained the European monarchs of old. Like the
nineteenth-century French liberals, Jouvenel emphasizes the reactionary as well as despotic character of allegedly modern and
democratic ideas. Both absolutist and democratic theories of
sovereignty "are constructed on the same intellectual model; they
confer the same despotic right on the effective wielder of power,
who is seldom the king, and can never, by the nature of things, be
the people" (s, 239). True liberalism, necessarily, takes aim at "the
principle of the unchecked and unbounded sovereignty of a human
will" (s, 239), whatever its source or justification. In particular, it does
not indulge the democratic conceit of the sovereignty of the people.

We have seen that Jouvenel was no apologist for the despotic
theories advanced by apologists for the Stuart and Bourbon mon-

archies in seventeenth- and eighteenth-century Britain and France. But he greatly admired the conception of limited or regulated sovereignty advanced by the jurists of the French old regime, a conception that he believed was in decisive respects renewed and revitalized by nineteenth-century French liberals. What, then, are the essential features of this alternative conception of sovereignty? To begin with, the jurists of the old regime in no way denied the need for a supreme authority within society. Without such an authority, a nation is vulnerable to invasion from abroad and to "misery, desolation and ruin" at home (s, 240). These partisans of ordered liberty believed that European monarchy was a time-honored means of maintaining public order while avoiding despotic rule. But the jurists of the French old regime did not believe that "every order which issues from a legitimate source is legitimate" (s, 240). They could not affirm this without also assenting to the impious claim that "there is no antecedent idea of justice" (s, 240) outside and above the positive law. This they refused to do. As Christians they firmly distinguished between just and unjust laws and refused to conflate lawful monarchy with arbitrary despotism. Jouvenel cites a remarkable passage from the *Maximes du droit public français*, published in Amsterdam in 1775, which expressly repudiates the "Hobbesian" claim that the sovereign is free to do as he pleases. The passage is sufficiently revealing to merit extensive citation:

> In order to attribute to the prince this unlimited authority, it is necessary to adopt the system of Hobbes, who knows no other rule of good or bad, just or unjust, than the civil laws; who regards as good everything which the prince commands and as

bad everything which he forbids. From this he concluded that
sovereigns are impeccable and can never rightly be blamed. Their
will makes the just and the unjust; therefore they can never en-
croach on what is another's because it becomes theirs the moment they want it.

How is it possible for them to act unrighteously? There is
nothing unrighteous except what they have forbidden because
they have forbidden it, and they forbid themselves nothing.
(quoted in s, 253)

The parliamentarians thus were acute critics of arbitrary rule
but they were far from being constitutionalists in the contemporary sense of that term. They placed few hopes in "institutional" or
"juridical" solutions to the pressing problem of politics in an old
regime monarchy: how does one prevent an all-powerful sovereign
"from willing what he ought not to will" (s, 242)? As a result, they
were willing to tolerate more authority in the hands of a single
ruler than modern constitutionalists would deem prudent or wise.
At the same time, they rejected all claims to "willful" rule by any
king or sovereign authority. It is at least arguable that they under-
valued the role that formal institutional restraints must play in
limiting the abuses of power. Modern democrats will no doubt be
disturbed by the fact that they had no fundamental objection to an
absolute authority that recognized the sovereignty of God and respected the laws of the land. The parliamentarians were not above
showering monarchs with obsequious praise (s, 243). But the great
merit of the monarchists of the old regime was undoubtedly their
refusal to identify absolute and arbitrary authority. They supported
moderate or tempered government and defended the independence

of the parliaments or courts against the encroachments of an aggrandizing crown. As the official "depositors" (i.e., registrars) of the law, they proudly refused to register royal decrees that they believed sullied the dignity of a lawful and Christian king. They resisted royal arbitrariness less in the name of "rights" and more out of fidelity to the vocation of Christian monarchy. Their assertion that "the king could do no wrong" (s, 245) has been widely misconstrued because we have long forgotten the moral assumptions underlying that claim. The parliamentarians explicitly denied the authority of the king's subjective will. Rather, the king could do no wrong precisely because no lawful king could will what was wrong and remain faithful to "the royal will." The parliamentarians insisted that "ill-conceived and capricious" (s, 248) decisions could never partake of the dignity and reasonableness of the royal will, properly understood.

In Jouvenel's view, we are so enamored today of seeing the problem of constitutionalism through the lens of "the separation of powers" that we have forgotten the crucial role that moral education must play in constraining and humanizing Power. Unlike the theorists of modern sovereignty, who recognized no law above the human will, the monarchists of the old regime bowed before the sovereignty of reason, a sovereignty "independent of every human will" (s, 252). They insisted that the true sovereign must, paradoxically enough, be "perfectly unfree" (s, 252), that he must humbly subjugate his own will to the permanent requirements of reason and justice. His counselors and jurists were obliged to aid him in that sacred task. To be sure, this doctrine of "the regulated will" could never be fully effective without the institutional restraints that are the great contribution of modern constitutionalism. As the distinguished historian Ran Halévi has brilliantly demonstrated, during the last half of the eighteenth century the old idiom of "moderation," with its emphases on the moral education of the king and the "parliamentary" exercise of judicial power, had been thoroughly reinterpreted in light of Montesquieu's doctrine of "the separation of powers."[31] This turn to a more exclusively institutional reflection on the need for "power to check power" entailed some progress of political understanding but at the cost of undermining the insights of the older tradition. Without an accompanying affirmation of the primacy of reason and the subordination of will, democratic politics is vulnerable to internal subversion.

For their part, the great nineteenth-century French liberals had the wisdom to constitutionalize the insights of the old French jurists while rejecting the Hobbesian identification of will and justice. Thinkers such as Constant, Royer-Collard, Guizot, and Tocqueville "trained the artillery of ideas onto a new arbitrariness" (s, 256) and recovered a proper sense of deference before a higher order of things. They affirmed both "the sovereignty of reason" and "the separation of powers." In his *History of the Origins of Representative Government in Europe*, Guizot explained how "in no possible case can will of itself confer upon the acts which it produces the character of legitimacy." Instead, acts derive their justification from their conformity "to reason, justice, and truth, from which alone legitimate power can spring."[32] *Sovereignty* builds on this penetrating and permanent insight while providing it with more philosophical depth. Jouvenel found ample confirmation of its validity in the tragic political experience of the twentieth century.

Conclusion

In *On Power*, Jouvenel laments the fact that, in modern times, "law has lost its soul and become jungle" (OP, 351). Hedonist, utilitarian, and rationalist conceptions and justifications of law are unable to do justice to its perennial elements or prevent its arbitrary manipulation at the service of rapacious interests and ideological causes. Law has become "ambulatory" (*mouvant*; OP, 343) because shorn of a foundation outside the battle of individual interests and wills. For a long time the great Declarations of Rights, such as those of the United States and France, provided a noble substitute for the natural law and reminded citizens of the law's majesty as well as the demanding requirements of the public good. But these declarations were built on the weakest philosophical foundations and gave way before intellectual doctrines that denied any transcendental source of rights and obligations. In *On Power*, Jouvenel speaks ominously of a "rationalist crisis" at the root of modern political upheavals. Reason, deprived of its traditional identification with objective morality, was spiraling towards its destruction. In response to that crisis, Jouvenel proposed a radical reconsideration of the adequacy of liberal doctrine in its dominant form. His renewed emphasis on the regulated will as the moral foundation of nonarbitrary government provided much-needed ballast for the liberal critique of totalitarian democracy. In later essays such as "The Principate" and "The Means of Contestation" (both originally published in 1965) Jouvenel continued to explore the problem of arbitrary power and the means of containing it.[33] But he would never again return to an extended philosophical examination of the moral and metaphysical foundations of human liberty. This may be related to Jouvenel's professional preoccupation with specifically economic and social-scientific questions throughout the 1960s and '70s. It may also indicate a partial change of emphasis or orientation on his part. In any case, part 3 of *Sovereignty* articulates a profound indictment of philosophical modernity as well as a unique and enduring synthesis of the best insights of traditionalist, Catholic, and liberal thought. Jouvenel convincingly argues that liberalism must sever its historical identification with what Solzhenitsyn has famously called "anthropocentric humanism" if it is to provide a coherent and compelling defense of human liberty and dignity. This may be Jouvenel's greatest theoretical insight. It is one of the many reasons why *Sovereignty* richly rewards continued contemplation a half century after its original publication.

CHAPTER FIVE

ECONOMICS AND THE GOOD LIFE

BERNARD CAZES HAS WISELY OBSERVED that there is something mysterious about Bertrand de Jouvenel's decision in the late 1950s to shift focus from the realm of political philosophy to the relatively uncharted waters of futurist speculation.[1] But Jouvenel's transition to the "art of conjecture" was marked by undeniable continuities as well as by a series of surprising new emphases and explorations. If his writings on political philosophy provided the theoretical foundation for his efforts to renew the idea of the "good life" within the conditions of modernity, his later, practically oriented writings set out to concretize this great moral imperative. As a graceful practitioner of the art of conjecture, Jouvenel continued to explore the means by which the good life could be preserved within the open, dynamic society, even if that concern was now refracted in a multiplicity of ways. As this chapter hopes to demonstrate, Jouvenel's writings on political economy provide an indispensable bridge between these two periods in his thought and thus help reveal the underlying unity of his variegated corpus.

It is tempting for students of Jouvenel's thought to assign his writings to the Left or to the Right depending on whether the French political thinker places more emphasis in any particular work on the negative externalities associated with excessive state intervention or the distortions introduced by unfettered market relations. By doing so, however, one risks politicizing the work of a great moralist and exaggerating the discontinuities within a remarkably consistent philosophical reflection on human nature and politics. It is arguably the case that Jouvenel leaned more to the center-Right in his writings as a political philosopher during the 1940s and '50s and more to the center-Left in his reflections as a futurist and ecologist during the 1960s and '70s (although his continuing emphasis on the indispensable moral prerequisites of the free society remained broadly congruent with the conservative liberal tradition of political philosophy). But such partisan readings of Jouvenel's texts are largely beside the point. Whether leaning a bit more to the Right or the Left, whether emphasizing the despotic propensities of state power or its indispensability to building a more humane future, Jouvenel maintained his critical distance from the dominant presuppositions of theoretical modernity. To cite the formulation of the political theorist Joseph Cropsey, Jouvenel belongs to that small group of independent souls whose analyses and criticisms of commercial society owe less to the Left or Right than to a "quasi-classical standpoint" that stands above the ideological contestation of modern intellectuals.[2] In the company of Plato, Plutarch, Seneca, St. Paul, and Rousseau, Jouvenel challenged the reigning assumptions of the "chrematistic" society, the society that uncritically identified the good life with the endless expansion of wealth and the satisfaction of any and all subjective human desires.[3]

But he did so in a characteristically dialectical manner, accepting the practical imperative of productivity in modern society while pointing out the serious objections to any simple identification of the "Productivist City" with the good life for human beings. Despite occasional shifts in his practical judgments and commitments, Jouvenel always remained a principled critic of theoretical individualism and political collectivism as well as a (qualified) partisan of a classical and Christian conception of what constitutes the good life for men and women. He rejected "moral relativism with regard to public choice" while remaining acutely aware that the "common good cannot be sought in methods which the model of a small society inspires."[4] In this chapter we will examine some of Jouvenel's principal writings in political economy in order to clarify his principled opposition to collectivism as well as his commitment to a dialectical conception of the good life that is possible within complex, modern societies.

Jouvenel and the Classical Liberal Tradition

Bertrand de Jouvenel never accepted the individualistic and utilitarian assumptions underlying nineteenth-century economic liberalism or modern welfare economics. But he shared the aversion of classical liberals to any pretensions of omnipotence on the part of the state and he articulated a remarkably compelling critique of modern collectivism on both moral and prudential grounds. It is not surprising, then, that many readers and critics have confused

Jouvenel's position with that of more familiar currents of economic and philosophical liberalism. Jouvenel was indeed a charter member of Friedrich von Hayek's Mont Pélerin Society, the worldwide organization of intellectuals and economists founded in 1947 to defend classical liberalism and the free-market economy against its "collectivist" critics.[5] Moreover, in 1954 Jouvenel contributed an essay titled "The Treatment of Capitalism by Continental Intellectuals" to Hayek's classic volume *Capitalism and the Historians*.[6] Through his active involvement in the Mont Pélerin Society during its early years, Jouvenel maintained close personal and intellectual ties with a range of classical liberal and libertarian economists and social theorists. Jouvenel is even mentioned affectionately in Milton and Rose Friedman's memoirs and to this day is widely identified as an antistatist thinker by the libertarian-minded, particularly in North America.[7]

But to view Jouvenel as fitting comfortably among classical liberals and libertarians is, if not wrong, certainly misleading. The mature Jouvenel feared the insatiable appetite of the Minotaur, the seemingly inexorable expansion of state power in modern times. But he also affirmed the legitimacy, even the dignity, of the state or the public realm, and he was much more interested in rejuvenating the tradition of constitutionalism than in positing imaginary libertarian alternatives to existing societies. In fact, the ultimate target of his criticism was the individualism that provided the common underpinning of both modern capitalism and socialism. He repeatedly points out that the theorists of modern capitalism and socialism were *frère-ennemis* who shared the same "productivist," utilitarian, and individualist assumptions. They were united in re-

jecting older classical and Christian accounts of the good life and
the good society. Their conflict, which was much more about means
than ends, concerned relatively superficial matters, from a philosophical point of view. For Jouvenel, twentieth-century collectivism was a symptom of a larger social crisis inaugurated by the failure of "rationalist individualism," a social philosophy that could
not give a coherent account of the restraints and obligations that
are essential components of decent public and private life. This
individualist ethos, which came to the forefront in the nineteenth
century, undermined the authority of intermediate social bodies
beholden to tradition and older forms of moral authority rather
than to individual consent. It thereby created social conditions that
were extremely hospitable to collectivism in its different forms.

Jouvenel went beyond establishing a dialectical connection
between individualism and collectivism. On the one hand, he ad-
monished nineteenth- and twentieth-century bourgeois elites for
losing sight of the special responsibilities that belong to those with
a privileged place in the social order. On the other hand, he did
not hesitate to criticize the relatively shallow conception of human
nature and society underlying the most influential currents of liberalism. Against both, he affirmed the social nature of man and
endorsed a vision of the good society rich in affections and "social
friendship."

In contrast, the dominant thrust of free-market philosophizing is individualistic, even radically individualistic. Classical liberal theorists typically posit the autonomy of the individual; their
libertarian descendants above all value unrestricted individual and
consumer choice as the true hallmarks of the free society. Similarly,

central to modern welfare economics is the (unexamined) identification of the satisfaction of human desires with the good life, an identification with roots in the political philosophy of Thomas Hobbes.[8] This conflation of the satisfaction of desires with man's good cannot help but trivialize moral experience. Moreover, it is based on a radically individualistic psychology that for all intents and purposes takes the survival and cohesion of the social order for granted.

In his impressive 1952 essay "The Idea of Welfare," Jouvenel appealed to the Rousseauian insight that the public good or general will can never be a "mere summation" of the "private advantages" of individuals within a particular social order (what Rousseau famously called the "will of all").[9] Every individual depends on "certitudes factual, legal, moral" that are "given to him by society" and are never simply reducible to private satisfactions or desires.[10] The maintenance of this common framework (and of the social affections informing it) has next to no place in the truncated psychology and political philosophy of modern individualism. In marked contrast, Jouvenel believed that one could not do justice to the authoritative character of the good society by reducing it to some "felicific calculus" that measured the public good by the sum of individual satisfactions, however arbitrarily or idiosyncratically defined. This sort of unabashed relativism struck him as more than a little barbaric. "That a society which we may assume to have maximized the sum of subjective satisfaction should, when we survey it as a whole, strike us as falling far short of a 'good society,' could have been foreseen by anyone with a Christian background or a classical education," Jouvenel wrote in his 1952 volume *The*

Ethics of Redistribution (46). Jouvenel's libertarian admirers tend to abstract from the classical and Christian presuppositions underlying his critique of collectivist economics and politics. They rightly discern in him a powerful critic of modern collectivism; they fail to appreciate that his critique of collectivism and state centralization is rooted in a much more fundamental rejection of the individualism at the heart of all distinctively modern thought. They do not acknowledge the immense spiritual chasm that separates Jouvenel's capacious appreciation of the social nature of man from the narrowly individualistic assumptions characteristic of public-choice theorizing. For his part, Jouvenel never reduces human motivation to the sole desideratum of self-interest: he is disheartened by a world where love and friendship are increasingly crowded out by an imperial conception of the human self. Public-choice theorists, in contrast, relish in denying both the reality and efficacy of disinterested or public-spirited human motivations.

Let us now turn to *The Ethics of Redistribution,* in which Jouvenel's "liberal" rejection of collectivism and his classical and Christian affirmation of the good society come together in a particularly fruitful way.

The Ethics of Redistribution

As we have indicated, contemporary readers of *The Ethics of Redistribution* tend to be most attuned to the antistatist features of Jouvenel's argument. This is not surprising given that this dimension of Jouvenel's book is most familiar to his largely conservative-minded American readership. In *The Ethics of Redistribution* Jouvenel argues that there is an integral connection between government efforts at redistribution of income (through tax policy and government subsidies) and the unprecedented centralization of state power (unprecedented, that is, for ostensibly free societies). He demonstrates that large-scale efforts at redistribution inevitably give rise to a new managerial class that usurps the salutary role of older aristocratic and bourgeois elites (ER, 76–77). In Jouvenel's view, this substitution is unlikely to be a happy one. He points out that the full-scale redistributionist state will not be able to fulfill the myriad social functions previously carried out by the older elites. Most particularly, the humanizing concerns of those elites will no longer find a place in the infinitely more homogenized society that results from redistributionist policies. The consequences will include a coarsening of taste and a general leveling of the social order (ER, 41–42). Jouvenel reminds his readers that even Karl Marx could not have pursued his researches on *Das Kapital* without the generous support made possible by Engels's untaxed profits (ER, 71). At the end of the day, the result of massive government efforts at redistribution will not be the transfer of income from the richer to the poorer classes but rather the "redistribution of power from the individual to the State" (ER, 72).

What is most noteworthy about this book is not so much its conclusions, as persuasive as they generally are, but rather the richness of the arguments that underlie them. Therein can be found Jouvenel's true originality as a social thinker and critic. A closer examination of *The Ethics of Redistribution* reveals that Jouvenel's critique of collectivism is anything but libertarian in spirit or inspiration.

Jouvenel begins his discussion by pointing out that he is not interested in the "borderline quarrel" (ER, 6) between those who assert that redistribution has a fundamental disincentive effect on the productive capacities of modern society and those who believe that it is compatible with continuing or even enhanced economic vitality. This conflict, as important as it is, involves "no fundamentals" (ER, 6). Rather, his deepest concern is with the "ethical aspect" of the problem. And in the process of presenting an "ethical" critique of the redistributionist project, Jouvenel raises truly radical questions about the modern project's fundamental identification of the good society with the fulfillment of individual desire and the promotion of indiscriminate consumption.

Jouvenel carefully distinguishes redistribution, agrarianism, and traditional forms of socialism. "Redistribution is not descended from socialism; nor can any but a purely verbal link be discovered between it and agrarian egalitarianism" (ER, 7). In the process of contrasting these three approaches to social reform, Jouvenel highlights the thoroughly modernist underpinnings of the redistributionist project. He also reveals "the inner contradiction" (ER, 14) at the heart of modern socialism and all other attempts to combine premodern appeals to fraternity with the productivist and utilitarian ethos at the heart of the modern project.

Agrarianism is, in Jouvenel's account, above all concerned with equalizing land assets. Far from wishing to abolish private property, its ideal is a "property-owning democracy" wherein the "supply of capital—in this case land—"is evenly spread out" (ER, 10). Jouvenel insists that agrarianism is more than an "archeological" (ER, 8) curiosity—it is, in fact, rooted in a deep-seated ethical im-

pulse that continues to resonate in the modern world. "The agrarian solution lies in the economic sovereignty of each several owner
on his well-delimited field, which is equal in size to that of his
neighbor" (ER, 11). Agrarians try to drain the various sources of
social antagonism by "minimizing the occasions in which men's
paths cross (ER, 11)." In modern times, this search for individual
and familial self-sufficiency, if taken to its limit, is inevitably utopian given the high level of interdependence that marks complex,
commercial societies. Yet advocates of land redistribution can find
powerful support for their proposals in the teachings of the Bible
and the premodern Western tradition generally. Agrarian claims
rest "upon age-old tradition" and appeal "to an ancestral feeling of
rightness" (ER, 8). In the first half of the twentieth century, the
agrarian principle played a major role in the political demands of
radicals and reformers in Russia, eastern Europe, and southern Italy.
The great English Catholic writer G. K. Chesterton reformulated
it as a doctrine ("distributism") to address the ills of a "proletarian-
ized" world. It is an approach that will continue to appeal to the
human desire for equitable social arrangements even if it finally
presupposes the existence of a "ruder" or more primitive state of
society. But in its acceptance of property and of the need for permanent barriers between individuals and families, it falls far short
of demanding the revolutionary creation of a new man. It is finally
more nostalgic than revolutionary. It will fail to satisfy those who
crave a radical transformation of the human condition. Modern
socialism, in contrast, learned from Rousseau that "social antagonism arises from 'objective situations'" (ER, 12). It singled out property as the principal source of social antagonism. The socialist so-

lution is properly revolutionary and entails nothing less than the "destruction of private property as such" (ER, 12).

Socialism, Ancient and Modern

Socialist thinkers invariably promise that the state will "whither away" once the alleged source of social antagonism has been abolished. In practice "it is clear for all to see that the destruction of private property has not done away with antagonisms or given rise to a spirit of solidarity permitting men to dispense with police powers" (ER, 13). Yet Jouvenel insists that the socialist ideal should not be "summarily dismissed" (ER, 14). To be sure, police socialism of the Soviet type is a monstrosity and has nothing to do with liberty or fraternal community. In reality, Soviet communism entailed an inhuman intensification and radicalization of the materialist premises underlying all of modern thought. As Jouvenel put it in a 1957 essay, the Soviets were so "enamored of the [economic] buildup achieved by the hated and despised capitalism" that they came to believe that "its speedy emulation justifies greater pressures upon men than was ever exerted under capitalism."[11] For Jouvenel, the only "leftist" critique of modern capitalism worth taking seriously was the one first put forward by Rousseau in his famous "Discourse on the Arts and Sciences" (1750), at least as that critique was reformulated by the likes of the nineteenth-century Swiss political economist J.-C.-L. Simonde de Sismondi. Sismondi fully acknowledged capitalism's "unquestionable achievements" in building up the productive capacities of society, but he questioned whether economic development *as an end in itself* contributed either to the happiness or moral well-being of men.[12] If Rousseau used his incomparable rhetorical gifts to thunder against "progress" *tout court,* the more responsible Sismondi advocated a more balanced approach to economic growth and social development than the one proposed by the doctrinaire advocates of laissez-faire political economy.

Jouvenel was deeply sympathetic to thoughtful versions of the critique of the commercial and growth-oriented society such as Sismondi's and drew considerable insight from Rousseau's forceful restatement of the classical case for an austere and self-limiting social morality. For all that, he was no partisan of either the premodern or modern version of the socialist ideal. But he freely acknowledged that socialism is able to work reasonably well when "material goods are shared without question *because* they are spurned" (ER, 14). Such was the Christian monastic ideal. In genuinely fraternal communities, social unity had its source in a common renunciation of the things of the world, a renunciation undertaken in the name of fidelity to a transcendent God. But modern socialism rejects the religious foundation of human brotherhood. It aims at social unity and communal solidarity on the basis of a radically materialist social ethic. Far from rooting social solidarity in a common "contempt for worldly goods," it "adheres to the fundamental belief of modern society that there must be ever more worldly goods to be enjoyed, the spoils of a conquest of nature which is held to be man's noblest venture" (ER, 15). The modern socialist ideal "is grafted on to the progressive society and adheres to this society's veneration of commodities, its encouragement of fleshly appetites and pride in technical imperialism" (ER, 15). Socialism, then, is finally torn by an insuperable "inner contradiction" between its rejection of egoism and self-interest, on the one hand, and its emphatic endorsement of the modern vision of "ever-increasing consumption" (ER, 15), on the other. In Jouvenel's estimation, the goal of a society "rid of its antagonisms and transformed into a city of brotherly love" (ER, 16) is attainable only in small communities that renounce the essential aim of modern society. Rousseau understood this perfectly well even if his *soi-disant* disciples such as Robespierre "tried to create his community of citizens under social conditions [i.e., the large, extended, commercial and "representative" nation-state] which, as Rousseau expressly stated, were incompatible with it." To his credit, Rousseau foresaw that "socialism's higher aspirations" would be doomed if it "accepted the general purpose of modern society" (ER, 16). Marx, in contrast, rather crudely identified the vocation of the human race with an intransigent dedication to the "conquest of nature." It is no accident, as the Marxists like to say, that communism culminated in a ruthless effort to achieve fraternity through state coercion. In addition, communism could never really compete with capitalism's more consistent support for the *individual* as well as the collective pursuit of well-being. Why should individuals indefinitely eschew "consumer satisfaction" when the goal of life is said to be the material betterment of the human condition (ER, 15)? The attempt to graft the "higher aspirations" of socialism onto the premises of the productivist society ended up creating a tyrannical version of the modern ideal without ever approaching the stated goal of social unity or human brotherhood. Modern socialism is an utterly contradictory social ideal, a cul-de-sac for men and societies.

The Moral and Political
Consequences of Redistribution

Redistributionism is equally modernist in its underlying assumptions. For one thing, it presupposes a quintessentially modern attitude toward poverty. In premodern societies, writes Jouvenel, "the discovery of poverty, coupled with the assumption of the impossibility of removing it" (ER, 19), caused a widespread "revulsion" against riches and luxury. Unlimited wealth and conspicuous consumption were the true scandals or sins in the eyes of the old moralists. As Jouvenel writes elsewhere, the great moralists of the premodern Western tradition were convinced that the irresponsible excitation of human desires and the unlimited pursuit of wealth only served to make men slaves to those desires. Moreover, it would inevitably lead already excessively avaricious men to seek tyrannical power over their fellow human beings. Convinced that the augmentation of wealth could only be achieved by the "exploitation of men by men" the classical moralists advocated self-limitation as the wisest course for men and societies. But the new pacesetting middle classes of England and other emerging liberal societies were committed to progress and the spread of modern civilization. Poverty "in the midst of plenty" (ER, 19) was a travesty that had to be eradicated through the development of industry and the coordinated efforts of the state. With redistribution, charity comes of age. It is transformed by and put at the service of the Promethean ambitions of modern man.

Jouvenel insists that a self-respecting society must do what is possible to care for the disadvantaged. This principle had always been apparent to every civilized human being and was only obscured by the dislocations that resulted from the industrial revolution and dogmatism of laissez-faire ideology. Only in the transition period between traditional society (where the church and extended family "redistributed goods") and the creation of the modern welfare state was the individual truly "left helpless in his need" (ER, 20).

As we have seen, Jouvenel was no doctrinaire liberal. He appreciated that "the destruction of neighborliness, of responsible aristocracies, and of Church wealth" (ER, 22) made it all the more imperative for the state to play a major role in providing for the needs of the poor. What he questions is the widely held conviction that redistribution is the best way to address the problem of poverty in the affluent society. Even more fundamentally, he believes that redistribution is at odds with other social objectives equally essential to the maintenance of a decent social order. In Jouvenel's view, redistribution inevitably leads to "a great shift in activities" (ER, 40) within society. A truly serious redistributionist policy, one committed to the establishment of draconian ceilings and floors on maximum and minimum incomes, would radically alter any society's character. It would debase even a modest lower-middle-class standard of life (ER, 28), and in all likelihood the production of high-quality goods would cease (ER, 41). Such a program of redistribution would further eliminate the class of people with "independent means," that segment of the population most responsible for the intellectual and cultural initiatives that define a civilized society (ER, 76–77). Last but not least, it would lead to a dangerous concentration of power in the hands of the state, a power no less dangerous if the authorities continued to be elected by the people. As Tocqueville famously warned in the penultimate chapter of volume 2 of *Democracy in America*, a "sort of regulated, mild, and peaceful servitude" could be readily combined "with some of the external forms of freedom."[13]

Finally and most fundamentally, Jouvenel rejects the view that "subjective satisfaction" is the measure of the good society; incomes must be seen as more than "means to consumer-enjoyment" (ER, 47). In his view, redistribution is the logical culmination of modern utilitarianism and "takes its cue wholly from the society it seeks to reform" (ER, 48). To be sure, Jouvenel rejects the premise that radical redistribution would do more for the average citizen than a social market economy wherein welfare measures deliberately eschew redistributionist goals. But his criticism of redistribution goes far beyond that important but secondary prudential consideration. Above all, Jouvenel criticizes advocates of redistribution for their extreme individualism and for their refusal to address seriously the question of the good life. *The Ethics of Redistribution* raises a host of serious questions that lie at the heart of Jouvenel's postwar political philosophy: How can the question of the common good speak to the concerns of the progressive or productivist society? How can one free it from its historic identification with classical and medieval politics and political thought? Jouvenel provides no ready-made answers to these questions. But if the question of the good life is to be confronted in a truly serious way, it is necessary to avoid both "reactionary" nostalgia for a past golden age and the even more problematic "progressivist" refusal to distinguish between higher and lower, nobler and baser instincts and aspirations.

The final paragraph of the first of the three lectures that constitute this book reveals Jouvenel's deep aversion to any social doctrine that dogmatically identifies the question of the common good with the indiscriminate satisfaction of human desires. Jouvenel writes:

> What is to be held against [the redistributionists] is not that they are utopian, it is that they completely failed to be so; it is not their excessive imagination, but their complete lack of it; not that they wish to transform society beyond the realm of possibility, but that they have renounced any essential transformation; not that their means are unrealistic, but that their ends are flat-footed. In fact, the mode of thought which tends to predominate in advanced circles is nothing but the tail-end of nineteenth-century utilitarianism. (ER, 48)

Jouvenel delivered the lectures collected in *The Ethics of Redistribution* at Cambridge University's Corpus Christi College in fall 1949, a time when England was in the process of embarking on a great and controversial experiment in "social democracy." His book was thus a *livre de circonstance* as well as an elegant exercise in political philosophizing. It was published only in English and was never reprinted in Jouvenel's lifetime. Jouvenel would later come to have some reservations about the book, perhaps because of changed political circumstances (explicitly redistributionist thinking clearly had lost much of its intellectual allure in the decades after 1949) or perhaps because with the passing of years he became somewhat more sympathetic to the positive role that government could play in addressing modern social problems. But it is important to recognize that Jouvenel in no way repudiated the central philosophical arguments and claims of his 1952 book. There is an immediately discernable continuity of themes, perspectives, and emphases between *The Ethics of Redistribution* and Jouvenel's major writings on political economy from the 1960s and '70s.

Jouvenel's Middle Way

This continuity is readily apparent in the essays "Efficiency and Amenity" and "A Better Life in an Affluent Society,"[14] published in English in 1960 and 1961, respectively, and reprinted in his influential 1968 collection *Arcadie: Essais sur le mieux-vivre*.[15] In these insightful and charming essays, Jouvenel clarifies the uniqueness of his approach to political economy. He distinguishes it from that of the ancient moralists, such as Tacitus, Polybius, and Plutarch, as well as from that of the "relativist school" that is "so powerful nowadays."[16] In opposition to the classical moralists with their stern denunciations of commerce and luxury, Jouvenel argues that modern man has no choice but to accept the very considerable risk entailed in the "pursuit of ever more goods and services."[17] There is no opting out of the modern adventure. But the choice of the progressive society must be made without illusions: "our wealth-mindedness brings us into conflict with many values which deserve respect."[18] We must not lose sight of the fact that "the imperative of productivity" necessarily entails "a reversal of all social values."[19] This stunning "transvaluation of values" must be confronted *en pleine connaissance de cause* and should not simply be taken for granted in the manner of modern economic science.

Decent human beings have always placed great value on social solidarity and on a pious attachment to the traditions and territory of one's fathers. But the successful operation of a modern commercial society demands "a double opportunism" on the part of its members in their respective roles as consumers and producers.[20] It demands utmost flexibility in producing for the satisfaction of desires, whatever their intrinsic merit, and a willingness to consume those goods, however frivolous or unnecessary, which are available at the lowest costs. The old virtues of "stability and faithfulness to the past" are increasingly dismissed as irrational obstacles to the maximization of economic productivity, to the growth of the gross national product.[21] But as the Gospel powerfully attests, man cannot live by bread alone (Matthew 4:4). Human beings are more than producers and consumers: they are also fathers, mothers, believers, citizens, and members of a host of inherited and chosen communities. It is impossible for self-respecting human beings to detach themselves from all temporal bonds in the name of the requirements of a self-sufficient and inexorable economic system and in exchange for the spiritually unsatisfying promise of a materialist cornucopia. Modern men are thus torn between that system of production and consumption which is inseparable from our prosperity and liberty and our recognition that as citizens and human beings we have a collective "interest in the quality of life [our] contemporaries lead."[22] This inevitable tension between our concerns as citizen-moralists and our roles as producer-consumers must be mitigated by wise social policy and responsible human action. But it cannot be overcome by irresponsible calls for revolutionary action or reactionary efforts to return to some illusory vision of communal harmony and social immutability. These are antisocial distractions that do nothing to humanize or civilize the productivist city (and in the case of totalitarian revolution, they only serve to introduce unprecedented forms of repression and tyranny).

Jouvenel's vision of the good life in an affluent society combines admirable sobriety with a manly rejection of servile fatalism and resignation. Jouvenel's own position is modern in its opposition to the ancient moralists' choice for the closed, austere city, and classical in its opposition to modern subjectivism and relativism.[23] The latter point is particularly important for understanding Jouvenel's distinctive approach to questions of political economy. Against the relativist school, Jouvenel rejects the identification of values with subjective preferences. Society has a vital interest in attempting to educate and elevate the tastes and preferences of its members. While "it is the proper function of the spiritual and moral teacher to show men the worthlessness of some of the things they do desire," this task cannot be safely or exclusively relegated to the private realm.[24] It is a legitimate concern of political economy, properly understood. Against the reigning assumptions of modern welfare economics, Jouvenel affirms "that the judgments we pass upon the quality of life are not mere expressions of individual fancy but tend to objective value, however approximately attained."[25] But he has no illusions whatsoever that the judgments we pass on the quality of human choices and desires can fundamentally transform an economic system that has an inexorable logic of its own.

Conclusion: Humanizing the Productivist City

Despite his adamant refusal to identify human happiness or the political common good with a single-minded dedication to the conquest of nature and the maximization of economic growth, Jouvenel rejected all revolutionary and apocalyptic responses to our modern situation. He maintained a principled distance from both "technomania," an excessive or inordinate attachment to technological progress, and "technophobia," the identification of technological progress with inevitable societal disaster.[26] In his later writings, he set out to explore how human beings might "civilize" industrial or postindustrial society, how its resources might be utilized to promote an "ordre du Mieux-Vivre," an order of well-being for man.[27] He fully appreciated that wealth creation would remain the central preoccupation of modern society even as he pleaded for more attention to be paid to the quality of life in productivist societies.[28] He persuasively argued that intellectuals and social scientists had paid perhaps inordinate attention to the problem of productivity and wealth creation while more or less neglecting the "progress of amenity" in prosperous societies.[29]

If Jouvenel rejected all forms of revolutionary utopianism, he recognized the importance of deferring to some positive vision of the good life to guide the task of humanizing and civilizing modern progress. Hence his profound debts to the classical and Christian traditions. The inclination of modern thought was to identify the good life with "the civilization of power." As a result, it had surprisingly little to say about the ends or purposes of human existence. As Pierre Manent has argued in *The City of Man,* philosophical modernity takes its bearings from "the flight from evil,"[30] from the effort to put an end to such discernible threats to human happiness as poverty, suffering, and even death. With few exceptions, the great modern political philosophers put forward no positive account of the *summum bonum* for men or societies.

Jouvenel therefore turned to the best of premodern thought (along with Rousseau) to help recover those experiences of affection, admiration, and amity that are at the foundation of any substantial conception of the human good. He advocated a balanced approach to economic and social development that explicitly aimed to turn the productive resources of modern societies toward the cultivation of those amenities that make lives whole and pleasant. Economic development needs to be put at the service of man and not the other way around. Human beings will only be happy and whole when their status as "sensitive, working and social being(s)" is fully acknowledged by those hoping to shape the direction of modern civilization.[31]

For all that, his "utopia" is a decidedly practical one: genuine respect for the nature of man requires that the external environment be preserved in a way that does as little damage as possible to the "sensitive" faculties of man. In addition, the workplace must be made as rewarding and challenging as possible, and a man's family, neighbors, and fellow citizens should aim to "arouse in him feelings of love and admiration."[32] This vision of a life truly worthy of man, of a society that does its best to preserve and cultivate the amenities of life, is the furthest thing from a blueprint for the construction of a new man or wholly unprecedented kind of society. Jouvenel rejected every form of collectivism and accepted the market society without either loathing or jubilation. But he believed that free men need to dream about the reconciliation of productivity and amenity if they are to have a fighting chance of moderating the opportunism that inevitably marks modern, commercial societies. As Dennis Hale and Marc Landy have eloquently put it, Jouvenel believed that it was imperative for economists and other social scientists "to broaden their horizons so that their science could include in a single glance not just the 'goods' of conventional analysis but the Good itself."[33]

We see then that Jouvenel's political science attempts to transcend the quarrel of the ancients and the moderns by bringing "old gods to a new city," in the fine phrase of Wilson Carey McWilliams.[34] His work renews the question of the good life against the modern complacency of both classical liberals and modern socialists. Because of his intransigent refusal to rest content with established ideological categories, Jouvenel remains one of the few truly responsible radical and countercultural political thinkers of the age.

CHAPTER SIX

THE SPECTER OF
BELLICOSE POLITICS

IN THE TRADITION OF classical political philosophy, Bertrand de Jouvenel affirmed the centrality of friendship to politics properly understood. As we have seen, he had no illusions about the possibility or desirability of returning to the closed classical city, and his works contain eloquent warnings against "primitivist nostalgia" in all its forms. But he adamantly rejected sociological approaches to politics that begin by reducing politics to a neutral procedure or framework for institutionalizing and managing conflict.[1] He did not doubt that conflict is an inescapable dimension of all political arrangements that allow for a modicum of free human initiative. But if politics "is essentially conflict, why respect the institutions" whose task is to manage and channel it (PT, 234)? Sociological approaches to politics provide no adequate answer to this question. Jouvenel, in contrast, rejects all approaches to politics that define it by the attempt to flee evil rather than by the affections that bind fellow citizens one to another. In his view, to truly do justice to the specificity of politics, one must *begin* with the primacy of the good: "what constitutes a people is a general feeling of amity" (PT, 237). A recognition of the existential primacy of the good is perfectly compatible with a realistic appreciation of its fragility— factional strife can all too quickly transform the good citizen's desire for civic peace and social friendship into enmity of the worst sort.

In his writings Jouvenel is preoccupied with the contrast between mild and bellicose politics and the movement back and forth between these two types of politics. In *The Pure Theory of Politics* Jouvenel writes: "War is a condition which may obtain with foreigners, but peace is the condition which must obtain between compatriots: that is a most ancient axiom of Politics" (PT, 235). For Jouvenel, the politics of the twentieth century was marked by a failed but feverish effort "to do away with war" (PT, 235). In light of this ongoing effort to pacify the human condition, "all too little attention has been given to the phenomenon that internal politics have become increasingly more warlike" (PT, 235). This chapter will explore Jouvenel's analysis of the fundamental and enduring contrast between mild and "angry bellicose Politics" (PT, 264). The "natural" oscillation between peace and war, amity and bellicosity that has defined political history has been radicalized and transformed in the modern age by theoretical doctrines and revolutionary movements that proclaim conflict and violence to be ends in themselves. We will explore Jouvenel's account of the political violence that, since the French Revolution, has undermined the civility and social affections that lie at the foundation of mild politics. And we will see that, rejecting progressivist illusions, Jouvenel reveals both the primacy and the fragility of the political good and limns a path for the recovery of the moral foundation of constitutional politics.

The Poison of Faction

In a chapter of *The Pure Theory of Politics* titled "The Team against the Committee" (PT, 228–41), Jouvenel provides an insightful phenomenological description of the ways in which determined minorities ("the team") attempt to sway the decisions of public authorities ("the committee"). At its outer limits, the team may go beyond ordinary political persuasion and pressure and resort to terrorism and other displays of belligerence. The same chapter contains Jouvenel's richest account of the threat that bellicose politics poses to decent civic life. In these pages, Jouvenel renews the classical philosophical critique of "faction" in politics. It is to that important discussion that we presently turn.

Jouvenel's definition of faction is straightforward enough: a faction exists when "some part of a people is joined together in a bellicose spirit against some other part" (PT, 236).[2] Jouvenel suggests that the premodern political tradition's opposition to faction reflects less its utopian opposition to social diversity than it does its salutary concern for the preservation of civic peace and friendship. "Militant members of a faction regard some of their compatriots with hostility, that is, as strangers" (PT, 237). The fomenter of factionalism "stands in direct contradiction to the classical understanding of the statesman's function, deemed to be the establishment, preservation and increase of amity between citizens" (PT, 237). Even an urbane, liberal-minded proponent of commercial modernity such as David Hume shared the classical tradition's loathing for those "founders of sects and factions" who set citizens at war with each other.[3] Jouvenel writes that Hume appreciated that "warring factions first ruin the climate of civility and ultimately bring down the form of government under which they have arisen" (PT, 238). Such was the experience of both the Roman republic and the Italian republics of the Middle Ages, examples that were once familiar to all politically literate men.

It must be emphasized that neither Hume nor Jouvenel opposes the natural and perfectly constructive efforts of men to "band together for a common purpose." Neither has the slightest sympathy for the Spartan-style homogeneity so admired by Rousseau. But while it is natural for human beings to "band together in pursuit of a common intention . . . it is deplorable that the *animus* which unites them should turn to 'animosity' against those who do not favor their purpose." And it is perfectly "detestable that they should develop bellicosity towards these compatriots" (PT, 238). Jouvenel knows that it is no simple matter to forbid "political activity which waxes angry, pugnacious and threatening" (PT, 238), as the example of Weimar Germany well attests. But the sorry political experience of the first half of the twentieth century ought to have taught defenders of liberal politics that "violence is poison to the body politic, which, once introduced, spreads and leads to convulsions" (PT, 239). Defenders of the liberal order need to be on guard against all manifestations of the revolutionary and totalitarian poisons. The worst illusion is to take the fragile acquisition of civic order for granted. Political science needs to reclaim the wisdom of the ancients: all human experience confirms that "change in political manners can also occur in the wrong direction" (PT, 240). That simple affirmation is, in Jouvenel's view, the beginning of political wisdom.

Jouvenel's liberalism is the furthest thing from the abstract, ahistorical liberalism produced by many academic theorists today. He writes about the history of Britain and Rome (Shakespeare's two great political test cases) with a sense of intimate familiarity. The English experience provides grounds for hope—the nation with the "most lurid record of political violence, the most numerous instances of authority won at the point of the sword" (PT, 240) transformed itself after 1688 into the very model of constitutional propriety, one informed by "exemplary mildness" (PT, 240). Roman history, alas, moved in the contrary direction. Political disputes, however vigorous, were for a long time conducted with civility and formality under the republic. This republican civility ended on "the evil day when raving Senators assaulted Tiberius Gracchus and caused the blood of the newly re-elected tribune to be spilt on the very Capitol." This crime "opened a horrible century" marked by terrible crimes—peace was only restored under the imperial rule of Octavius. "[B]ut political criminality was to reappear at the very court of the emperors" (PT, 240). The Roman case is a sobering reminder of the possibilities of political degeneration and the evil consequences of the unleashing of full-scale political bellicosity.

Jouvenel's reflections on British and Roman political history were, of course, reinforced by his own experience of what he called "a political milieu . . . rife with political occurrences" (PT, xix). He came of age in an era where the political stakes were extremely high. In the age of totalitarianism, no one could afford to take the triumph of liberal civilization for granted. Yet much of contemporary political theory has been oblivious to this lesson. In "The Principate," Jouvenel observes that "the lessons learned from the Napoleonic experience had then brought almost the entire world of letters to 'constitutionalism,' to a belief in institutions that limit personal rule."[4] Jouvenel had in mind such eminent political thinkers as Benjamin Constant, who meditated on all the conclusions to be drawn from the experience of the French revolutionary terror and Napoleonic despotism. "It is very strange that the experience of Hitler—and how much worse *that* was!—did not start a similar movement!" exclaims Jouvenel, with justice.[5] Jouvenel's own political science, in contrast, aims to free liberalism from historicist complacency and to remind free men of what is truly at stake when a mild politics gives way to a politics of a more ferocious variety.

The Manners of Politics

Jouvenel's fullest exploration of the antithesis between mild and bellicose politics is found in "The Manners of Politics" (PT, 242–64), the penultimate chapter of *The Pure Theory of Politics*. This chapter is a gem of political reflection, richly displaying the urbanity and erudition that marks nearly every page of Jouvenel's corpus. In it, Jouvenel evokes the mild and polished political manners of an older Europe and traces how they came under increasing assault in the nineteenth and twentieth centuries from modern revolutionaries and various doctrinaires of extremist politics. Jouvenel draws an illuminating contrast between a mannered world where the stakes of politics were truly limited and an ideological age (beginning with the French Revolution but culminating in the tyrannies of the twentieth century) where the life and liberty of men were the very stakes of the political "game."

Jouvenel suggests that political manners are a powerful means for sustaining civic concord, for preventing the conflict inherent in political life from escalating into full-scale civic strife. Manners are an essential instrument of civic comity, and the introduction of brutish mores is the surest way of destroying the affections that bind citizens together. Manners are indispensable precisely because political conflict is a permanent feature of political life. A respect for decorum and civil conduct serve as a valuable reminder that political partisans on all sides are members of the same civic community.

Political conflict is ineradicable because human beings are bound to disagree about both "personal wants" and the meaning of the common good. Even when citizens sincerely pursue the common good serious disagreements arise. "The common good is indeed a powerful notion, but one of indefinite content" (PT, 244). Decent men will inevitably disagree both about its contents and its requirements. Conflict is thus rooted in the inevitable clash of interests and diverse conceptions of justice that characterize any free and dynamic political community. It is utopian to think that some rational plan for a good society or a priori conception of the common good can be imposed on all-too-recalcitrant human beings. Such efforts are bound to culminate in tyranny. In light of these realities, the good citizen learns to moderate his expectations and to search for more or less provisional "settlements" to enduring political problems (PT, 245, 265–76). In a decent political order, it is imperative for participants in the game of politics to do nothing to unnecessarily exacerbate its potentially dangerous stakes.

For Jouvenel, nineteenth-century England offered the prototype of mild politics. He writes almost wistfully about its virtues:

> The game of Politics in its parliamentary guise obtained a good reputation thanks to its manners in nineteenth-century England. Neither the players nor third parties stood to lose from the game. Whatever its fortunes, the governance of England altered very little and always in the direction of improvement. Citizens had no cause for alarm: they feared nothing from Government, whatever category they belonged to; neither did they look to government for any sudden change in their condition. (PT, 246)

Such were the conditions of political life in a constitutionalist England that had successfully withstood the virus of revolutionary politics and had not yet been fully transformed by the requirements of democratic legitimacy. Jouvenel turns to Anthony Trollope's novel *The Prime Minister* to illustrate the mores of a social order wherein the stakes of politics are truly moderate. English parliamentary politics demanded "decorous conduct" (PT, 247) and a scrupulous regard for the rules of the game. No one was particularly worse off for failing in politics and no one lost his life in the pursuit of a political career. Trollope's hero, the Duke of Omnium, has a passion for public life and a fear of political failure. Yet he knows that defeat in politics will not affect anything of ultimate value to him. When Omnium's cabinet falls, Lady Glencora asks him if he feels like Wolsey or Plantagenet. The Duke's lapidary response is quite telling: "Not in the least my dear. No one will take anything from me which is my own" (quoted in PT, 248).

Jouvenel incisively comments on this exchange:

> How true! And how right is Trollope to point the lesson by reference to the persecution of the fallen Wolsey! The Duke of Omnium has won and lost the Premiership; but as he goes out, he is assured of retaining his liberty, property and status. And this safety of *res privatae* from the vagaries of Politics is enjoyed by every inhabitant of the realm: no one is going to suffer from the fall of the government just as no one suffered from its advent. (PT, 248–49)

But political moderates in Weimar Germany did not have the luxury of opting for arrangements in which the stakes of the game of politics were moderate. Hitler made "civil liberties and the lives of the Jews" (PT, 246) the stakes of his particular game of dice. The diabolical consequences of his victory would only become fully apparent with time. However, the radicalization of the stakes of politics did not begin with twentieth-century tyrants such as Hitler. According to Jouvenel, its roots can be found in the French revolutionary assault on mannered and civil politics. It was this momentous event that opened up an era of political violence, violence increasingly sanctioned—even sanctified—by theory.

Jouvenel observes that such diverse observers as Jacques Necker (the chief minister during the initial period of the revolution and an advocate and architect of reform), Edmund Burke, and Benjamin Constant were equally appalled by the French Revolution's "proscription of civility" and its accompanying unleashing of "brutal language, loutish familiarity, and gross irreverence" (PT, 251). Jouvenel tellingly remarks that this brutal disregard for civility paved the way for the Terror, since "the man who prides himself on not sparing the feelings of his fellows in his language will pretty soon not mind inflicting more concrete injuries" (PT, 252). The brutal mores that accompanied the revolution "came as a surprise to Europe. All expected political change: none the new expressions on faces, the new tone of voices" (PT, 252). A postrevolutionary liberal such as Constant hoped to separate the positive achievements of the revolution (such as civic and legal equality) from its terroristic disregard for human life and constitutional formalities. Writing at the beginning of the revolution, Burke condemned it *tout court,* swayed in no small part by its "subversion of civility" (PT, 252). Jouvenel recounts the role that the brutishness of the mobs and the assault on the royal family on October 6, 1789, played in shaping Burke's violent reaction to the revolution:

> Episodes are telling: when the mob marched to Versailles and carried the Royal family with it by mere pressure of force, when the heads of guards, carried on spears, were kept bobbing up and down at the window of the Queen's carriage, this outrage, both to formality and to sensitivity, was one which the deputies dared not condemn, and it is apparent in Burke's writing that such a scene and its condoning by the assembly swayed him altogether. (PT, 252)

Jouvenel's treatment of "the manners of politics" is profoundly indebted both to Burke's positive endorsement of decorous politics as well as to his searing critique of French revolutionary brutality. It is easy to dismiss Burke's long tribute (in *Reflections on the Revolution in France*) to the young Marie Antoinette as evidence of his conservative romanticism. But it is important to remember that Burke's defense of "the pleasing illusions, which made power gentle" is a perfectly *reasonable* one.[6] In his view, European chivalry had tied manliness to gentleness and had "subdued the fierceness of pride and power."[7] In Christian Europe, authority had been tamed by elegance and "subdued by manners." But modern rationalist philosophy, vulgarized by the revolutionaries, had no place for taste, elegance, or even moral self-restraint. Its cold, calculating rationality undermined the "love, veneration, admiration, or attachment" that connect people to their commonwealth.[8] The reason of the revolutionaries, oscillating in practice between sentimentality and brutality, "banished the affections" but was "incapable of filling their place."[9] In Burke's view, public affections, combined with manners, are required as "supplements," "correctives" and "aids" to the law.[10] Otherwise politics becomes a thinly disguised form of war. Burke movingly reports that "as a prince" Louis XVI felt "for the strange and frightful transformation of his civilized subjects,"[11] as evidenced by the atrocious spectacle of October 6. Burke articulated this transformation more vividly and intelligently than any other critic of the revolution. He knew that the French Revolution had opened a frightening episode in European—and world—history. It had not only put an end to the remnants of the ancient constitution of Europe; it had also, in Jouvenel's striking words, left "another inheritance": "it . . . hallowed violence" (PT, 253). If Constant and Tocqueville learned from the revolutionary excesses the need for an uncompromising commitment to political moderation, other less wise voices would come to proclaim not only the necessity but the *sublimity* of revolutionary violence. As a result, the twentieth century would come to experience political violence on a scale hitherto unimaginable.

The Sanctification of Violence

Jouvenel observes that while "the history of political messianism has been well written . . . we lack a parallel history of the sanctification of political violence" (PT, 254). In "The Manners of Politics," Jouvenel sketches just such an account. He begins by highlighting a series of prominent writers and theorists who provided influential "aesthetic" defenses of the sublime possibilities inherent in extreme actions. Inspired by the bloody example of the French revolutionaries, these writers came to identify heroism with cruelty, violence with vitality, and moral obtuseness with true courage. Jouvenel provides a compelling account of the role that such "aesthetic suggestions" (PT, 254) played in the overcoming of "the natural sense that [violence] is wrong" (PT, 254). But in my view Jouvenel's discussion of political violence is marred by a failure to adequately account for the interaction of utopian ideologies with the perverted aesthetic sensibility that made violence attractive to so many thinkers and actors in the first place. In fact, at one point he explicitly denies that "messianic" political hopes— or "intellectual error" of any sort—had much to do with the revolutionary intensification of political violence (PT, 254). This relative neglect of ideological utopianism is a major lacuna in Jouvenel's thought. If terrorism and tyranny ultimately depend on "the complete abolition of moral sense" (PT, 234), as Jouvenel rightly suggests, then only ideological justifications, rooted in intellectual error, can provide the rationale for the suspension of the moral law. Jouvenel's description of the sanctification of political violence since the French Revolution illuminates part, but only part, of the "transvaluation of values" in modern times. His narrative of the history of political violence needs to be supplemented by a fuller account of the role of ideology in justifying modern terror and tyranny.

Jouvenel concentrates on two principal examples of the "new 'sublim[ity] of extreme actions'" (PT, 254). The first is the "micro-portrait" of Julien Sorel in Stendhal's *Le rouge et le noir* (PT, 254). "In a succession of small incidents, Julien overcomes both his timidity and his decency, which he satanically confuses, to do the bold thing." Jouvenel reads the book as an "apology of criminality for its own sake" (PT, 255). *Le rouge et le noir* culminates in one final and daring criminal act: through the gratuitous act of killing his mistress, Julien rises above himself and finds a kind of pathological fulfillment. Jouvenel notes that this defense of violence for its own sake would find a later echo in André Gide's defense of the "gratuitous act" in *Les caves du Vatican* (PT, 255). Such "vitalistic" justifications of violence would play no small part in undermining the deeply ingrained human sense that acts of gratuitous cruelty are inherently evil.

Jouvenel next turns to Georges Sorel's comparatively unknown *Reflections on Violence* (1908) for his other principal illustration of the theoretical defense of violence. Jouvenel argues that Sorel "stands at the beginning of the twentieth century as its herald" (PT, 255).

This moralist of violence denounced the hold that obsolete notions of natural law and conscience still had on the minds of men
even as he celebrated violence as an indispensable means for invigorating a decadent civilization and overcoming social injustice.
He incessantly mocked liberals, humanitarians, and peacemakers.
Jouvenel contrasts Marx's "bourgeois" view of violence as a means
to "overcome irrational behavior" (PT, 255) with Sorel's positive
celebration of violence both as an end in itself and as a means of
moral and social transformation. The transformative violence that
Sorel found in the general strike of the anarcho-syndicalists had
little in common with the Marxian confidence that mankind was
ultimately proceeding toward a final state of pacification and reconciliation.

Sorel proposed a powerful synthesis of Marxist proletarian violence and proto-Nietzschean pessimism and vitalism. Jouvenel is
not wrong to suggest that this fusion of socialism and aesthetic
vitalism played an important role in shaping the revolutionary spirit
of the twentieth century. One thinks of Sartre's *Critique of Dialectical Reason*, published one year after *Pure Theory*, where the same
fusion of Marxism and a quasi-fascistic celebration of violence can
be found.[12] Many other expressions of Sorelian-style vitalism can
be found in the writings and utterances of the New Left defenders
of revolutionary violence. The intellectual partisans of Mao and
Castro in the 1960s and '70s undoubtedly owed as much to the
spirit of Sorel as to the theoretical ratiocinations of Karl Marx.

For Sorel, writes Jouvenel, the proletariat may have been "the
chosen" people, but ultimately the "specific content" of revolutionary politics was less important than the imperative of violence

itself (PT, 256). About this Jouvenel is surely right. As evidence, he points to the fact that Sorel would come to applaud both Lenin and Mussolini. Sorel welcomed revolutionary assaults on bourgeois democracy from both the Left and the Right. Jouvenel does not mention the very interesting fact that the fourth edition of *Reflections on Violence* concludes with an appendix titled "In Defense of Lenin." There Sorel praises Lenin as "the greatest theoretician that socialism has had since Marx" and argues that as a head of state Lenin's "genius recalls Peter the Great."[13] It is immediately evident that Sorel knew next to nothing about the real character of Leninist socialism: he identifies it with the victory of the very soviets that the centralizing Lenin was in the process of eviscerating. No matter: Lenin was an enemy of a bourgeois civilization that was beyond repair and his methods were "Sorelian" to the core.

Jouvenel's account of the sanctification of violence since the French Revolution clarifies crucial features in the development of bellicose politics. It also allows us to more fully appreciate the respectability of the choice for violence among European intellectual elites that had been achieved by the start of the twentieth century.

Yet something is missing from this otherwise rich account. We have already spoken about Jouvenel's failure to adequately integrate the intellectual and aesthetic features of modern tyranny and terror. An examination of Jouvenel's 1963 essay "On The Evolution of Forms of Government" reveals just how far he went in denying a central role to Marxism in the genesis of modern totalitarianism. It is to Jouvenel's perplexing deemphasis and instrumentalization of ideology that we now turn.

Ideology and Modern Tyranny

In "On the Evolution of Forms of Government" Jouvenel draws a sharp contrast between the optimistic assessment of the future of parliamentary government proffered by many European liberals before and immediately after the end of the Great War and the tragic itinerary of European politics after 1918.[14] After the devastating experience of total tyranny in the first half of the twentieth century, he writes, it is no longer excusable to confuse the normative superiority of liberal politics with a "factual" judgment about its inevitable triumph.[15] Such progressivist illusions are clearly unwarranted.

Jouvenel concentrates on the revealing case of Edward Benes, the Czech statesman for whom Jouvenel had worked as a private secretary in the early 1920s. Benes was the prototype of a humane, liberal-minded statesman who falsely presupposed that liberal democracy was "the preordained *terminus ad quem* of political evolution."[16] Benes believed that the collapse of the Habsburg, Hohenzollern, and Romanov dynasties at the end of the First World War augured well for the future of self-government and self-determination in Europe. He was even confident that Russia's new Bolshevik rulers would eventually come to appreciate the value of parliamentary and legal freedoms. With the help of a properly constituted international authority such as the League of Nations, Benes was certain that the world would move forward toward a bright democratic future. He was, of course, to be sadly disappointed. He lived to see the establishment of militarized tyrannies in Italy and Germany, the entrenchment of totalitarian terror in the old Rus-

sian empire, and the gradual displacement of all democratic regimes by authoritarian ones in east-central Europe (with the admirable exception of his own Czechoslovakia). With Munich in 1938,
Benes, by then the president of Czechoslovakia, would witness the
ultimate act of political dishonor, the abandonment of Czech democracy to Nazi imperialism by his nation's erstwhile French and
British allies. In 1948, he would stand by impotently as a communist coup d'état brutally imposed Stalinist tyranny on his country.
He would die a broken man, his illusions shattered, a witness to
the changing fortunes of European liberty in the twentieth century.

The example of Benes is most instructive. Jouvenel greatly
admired this decent and civilized man. He fully shared Benes's commitment to mild, humane politics. But Benes's political judgment
was too informed by the historicist self-confidence of pre-1914
Europe. Jouvenel was the product of a quite different milieu, one
that witnessed the rise of unprecedentedly virulent tyrannies and
the thoroughgoing militarization of politics. In "On the Evolution
of Forms of Government" Jouvenel quotes the great French an-
thropologist Marcel Mauss about the "conspiratorial" ethos that
he witnessed among revolutionary political circles at the beginning
of the twentieth century:

> I have long lived in the circles of the active Russian P.S.R.; while
> I had less to do with the social-democrats, I well knew the Bol-
> sheviks of the Parc Montsouris and indeed I have lived with
> them somewhat also in Russia. The activist minority was a real-
> ity there: it was an unrelenting conspiracy. This went on through
> the war and under the Kerensky Government which it finally

vanquished. But the form of the Communist Party has remained that of a secret sect, and its essential organ, the GPU, is the combat team of a secret society. The Communist Party itself remains camped in Russia, as the fascist and Hitlerian parties also camp, without artillery or fleet, but with a police apparatus.[17]

The radical revolutionary movements that would come to power in Russia, Italy, and Germany between 1917 and 1933 treated their citizens like enemy belligerents in conquered territory. The old distinction between domestic and foreign politics, between the bellicosity that is *sometimes* appropriate in foreign affairs and the amity appropriate to domestic political life, was completely effaced. The totalitarian party-states of the twentieth century camped on enemy territory, in perpetual search for "enemies of the people." Jouvenel fruitfully draws on Élie Halévy's powerful account of the rise of Communist and fascist tyrannies in his 1938 classic, *The Era of Tyrannies*.[18] In that work, Halévy describes the way in which the mass mobilization of society, in particular "the organization of enthusiasm" and the collectivization of production in Germany during World War I, provided an inspiration and precedent for Lenin's totalitarian experiment. Rathenau's "war socialism" provided a model for Lenin's "war communism," establishing the feasibility of the militarization and mobilization of an entire society. And Lenin's tyranny in turn provided a model of tyrannical rule that was readily exploited by anticommunist tyrants who rejected liberal democracy in the name of national grandeur. Jouvenel recognizes that the tyrannies of the twentieth century could not survive without ideological justification. But he tends to see such justification as *instru-*

mental to the larger purpose of societal mobilization. For the most part he argues that the militarization of society is an end in itself for those committed to a revolutionary adventure. Following Halévy, Jouvenel doesn't hesitate to identify Communist and fascist tyrannies, to emphasize the debt that fascism owed to the Soviet model, or to point out the striking similarities between Communist and fascist mores and techniques of governance. Both writers deserve much credit for their lucidity about the nature of the new tyrannies of the Left and Right.

Jouvenel and Halévy both admit that "the new tyrants have a new justification for unlimited and uncontrolled power: it is required for the fulfillment of purpose."[19] But this point has something of the character of an afterthought: neither man sufficiently emphasized the fact that, at least at the beginning of their adventures, revolutionary elites were intensely committed to their respective ideological justifications. And these ideological justifications were more than justifications—they were in fact powerful motives for thought and action. Both Halévy and Jouvenel overstate the ways in which violence and brutal mores are ends in themselves and understate the ways in which ideological faith, messianic hopes, allow men to move mountains. Both are hesitant to replace a promising critique of tyranny with what Jouvenel calls a "largely irrelevant" critique of Marxism.[20]

Jouvenel often remarks that Marx's libertarian hopes for a decentralized socialist society had little in common with the hypercentralized reality of Soviet-style communism (although he would reluctantly concede in his last major work, *Marx et Engels*, that Marx bore some responsibility for the despotisms that had been inaugurated in his name).[21] But Marx's dream of a libertarian utopia at the end of history was unthinkable without the revolutionary displacement of bourgeois democracy by a "dictatatorship of the proletariat." "Totalitarianism" and "libertarianism" are two complementary moments in Marx's thought. Marx despised representative institutions, scorned "formal freedoms," and welcomed the violence associated with the Paris commune. He dreamed of a world without conflicts and divisions, an inherently utopian goal that demanded tyrannical methods in its pursuit. Leszek Kolakowski more accurately suggests that Marxist-Leninism is a *legitimate* interpretation of the political consequences of Marx's Marxism, if not the only possible one.[22]

In my judgment, an adequate account of modern tyranny must openly confront the central role of Marxism as an inspiration and justification for bellicose politics. In a famous passage in *The Gulag Archipelago*, Aleksandr Solzhenitsyn highlights the crucial role that ideology, including Marxist-Leninism, played in allowing modern tyrants to ignore age-old moral limits with seeming impunity. This passage clarifies both the nature and deadly consequences of ideological justification:

> To do evil, a human being must first of all believe that what he's doing is good, or else that it's a well-considered act in conformity with natural law. Fortunately, it is in the nature of the human being to seek a *justification* for his actions.
>
> Macbeth's self-justifications were feeble—and his conscience devoured him. Yes, even Iago was a little lamb too. The imagination and the spiritual strength of Shakespeare's evildoers stopped short at a dozen corpses. Because they had no *ideology*.

Ideology—that is what gives evildoing its long-sought justification and gives the evildoer the necessary steadfastness and
determination. That is the social theory which helps to make
his acts seem good instead of bad in his own and other's eyes, so
that he won't hear reproaches and curses but will receive praise
and honors. . . .

Thanks to *ideology*, the twentieth century was fated to experience evildoing on a scale calculated in the millions. This
cannot be denied, nor passed over, nor suppressed.[23]

Jouvenel cannot be said to have ignored the ideological features of
modern tyranny. He appreciated the "teleocratic" character of
modern regimes and adamantly rejected all ideological justifications of terror and tyranny.[24] In "The Team against the Committee" Jouvenel writes that a member of a "team" that opts for a
terroristic assault on legitimately constituted authority can do so
only because he is "obsessed by an 'idée fixe,' an intention, deemed
moral, which he pursues at all costs. The most immoral of all beliefs
is the belief that it can be moral to suspend the operation of all moral
beliefs for the sake of one ruling (supposedly moral) passion" (PT,
234). It is this immoral belief that allows for "the complete abolition
of the moral sense" which is necessary for totalitarianism and terror
to do their work. Jouvenel adds this striking comment: "this
precisely is the doctrine which has run throughout the twentieth
century" (PT, 234). These remarks ably capture the nature of
ideological justification and its crucial role in obfuscating the
natural moral sense of human beings. They complement
Solzhenitsyn's analysis in *The Gulag Archipelago*. But Jouvenel does
not truly integrate his brief and penetrating discussion of ideologi-

cal justification into his larger history of political violence. That task is left for others to complete.

Conclusion: The End of History?

One of the great merits of Jouvenel's political science is the way it conveys the notion of the fragility of civilized or mild politics to an age that is all too prone to genuflect before the altar of progress. Jouvenel frees liberalism from historicist complacency and reminds his readers of unpleasant political possibilities that they would prefer to ignore. It is tempting to dismiss Jouvenel as a pessimist whose judgment was distorted by the exceptional events (total war and total tyranny) that he witnessed in his lifetime. In this reading, Jouvenel's purported pessimism would be just as much a product of his time as was Benes's naïve confidence in the inevitable triumph of parliamentary liberalism. But such a reading would be superficial. Jouvenel's deeply held conviction that political change can occur in the wrong direction does not simply reflect an unwarranted universalization of the parochial experience of a European caught up in the tragedies of the twentieth century. No doubt the tragic unfolding of unprecedented forms of tyranny in the twentieth century profoundly shaped Jouvenel's conviction that the worst is always possible in politics. But this judgment was reinforced by, and grounded in, his study of political philosophy and history. His reading of Aristotle, Thucydides, Cicero, and Shakespeare, his reflection on British and Roman history, and his own experience of the darkest political storms cured him of progressivist illusions. There was finally nothing parochial, nothing narrow, about the quality of Jouvenel's political reflection.

Jouvenel died in 1987 and therefore did not live to reconsider his analysis in light of the collapse of communism in Eastern Europe between 1989 and 1991. But nothing suggests that Jouvenel would have retrospectively dismissed "the era of tyrannies" as a mere anachronism, a slight detour on humankind's forward march toward rational modernity. This was the erroneous judgment that Auguste Comte and Benjamin Constant had both made about the French revolutionary terror and Napoleonic despotism. Jouvenel was alert to their mistake and would not have repeated it after the far more destructive totalitarian episode. Comte and Constant believed that "usurpation and conquest" were irrational in the "age of commerce," in the "industrial society" that had superseded the "military societies" of the past. In "The Manners of Politics," Jouvenel persuasively argues that such thinking was based on a faulty premise, on an unfounded "bourgeois postulate" (PT, 259) that presupposed that violence was always a means to material ends. If that were the case, then "civilized calculation" would indeed demand the rejection of violence as a rational instrument of politics.[25] Jouvenel certainly agreed that societies that wish to promote the material well-being of their citizens would be better off pursuing the peaceful path of commercial modernity than the less productive methods of pillage and conquest. But men and communities fight not only to gain material advantages but also for glory, ideas, and even for the excitement that accompanies the unleashing of violence. There is no reason to think that human nature itself is unquestionably "bourgeois," that other human motives and possibilities are wholly obsolete in the modern age.

We have now entered a new era of mild politics that is accompanied by new forms of historicist complacency. To be sure, the democracies—many of them, anyway—are presently at war with fierce terrorist enemies, Islamist fanatics who reject the very idea of moderate politics. But most Europeans and Americans no longer truly fear the possibility of despotism reoccuring among what Comte labeled the "avant-garde of humanity." We have already come to think of totalitarian tyranny as an accident, an anachronism, an event of merely historical importance. Jouvenel, in contrast, encourages us to widen our political imaginations in order to confront the full range of political possibilities. He reminds us that "the mildness of politics is not so well assured, that its maintenance needs to be contrived: that this indeed is the first and foremost of political arts" (PT, 241). As a result, the serious reader of Jouvenel is immunized against "naïve fable(s) of the happy arrival at the 'end of history.'"[26] For that, we have every reason to be grateful.

CHAPTER SEVEN

POLITICAL PHILOSOPHER AND "VOYAGER IN THE CENTURY"

BERTRAND DE JOUVENEL MAY HAVE BEEN one of the outstanding political philosophers of the twentieth century, but he was not always a trustworthy guide to the practical politics of that contentious era.[1] In the 1930s, he despaired of liberal democracy and oscillated between equally irresponsible leftist and rightist political options. For a time, he flirted with socialism and supported the "Popular Front" of Socialist, Radical, and Communist parties in France. As we have seen, Jouvenel conducted a now infamous interview with Hitler in February 1936 in which he did not challenge the German tyrant's self-presentation as a statesman intent on preserving the European peace and bringing about the economic and social renewal of his country. As if to highlight the unreliability of Jouvenel's political judgment, the unfortunate interview was published in *Paris-Midi* on the eve of the German remilitarization of the Rhineland, an act undertaken in complete disregard of the Treaty of Versailles and Germany's existing international obligations. Jouvenel rightly felt humiliated for having allowed himself to be manipulated by a cunning despot. It is not that Jouvenel harbored any ideological sympathy for the National Socialist revolution or ever abandoned his commitment to free political institutions. But he was understandably disturbed by the slow, uncertain response of the democracies to the scandal of mass unemployment (Jouvenel once told an interviewer that unemployment was "the only subject about which I am fanatical").[2] As a result, he was somewhat complacent toward those individuals or regimes who were doing something, anything, to address the social crisis engulfing the Western world. As Eric Roussel has suggested,[3] the Jouvenel of the mid-1930s failed to adequately distinguish between the "energetic and experimental"[4] social measures pursued by a democratic reformer such as Franklin Delano Roosevelt (whom Jouvenel admired profoundly at the time) and the totalitarian "solution" to unemployment and social instability introduced by Hitler in Germany after 1933. Jouvenel succumbed to impatience and lost confidence in the ability of liberal parties and regimes to act swiftly and deal adequately with the social crisis that defined this epoch. His subsequent return to the old liberal verities resulted from his bitter experience of tyranny and total war and accounts for the pathos that informs nearly every page of *On Power*.

The interview with Hitler was not the only example of Jouvenel's unsteady judgment in the 1930s. In 1936 Jouvenel joined Jacques Doriot's extremist Parti populaire français (PPF) and followed this rightist demagogue right up until the Munich Pact in the fall of 1938. But Jouvenel's commitment to Czech independence (solidified by his longtime association and friendship with

Benes) and his solicitude for political liberty kept him from succumbing to the totalitarian temptation. Aside from questionable
contacts with his old friend Otto Abetz, the German representative in Paris after June 1940, Jouvenel conducted himself honor-
ably during the occupation, joining the resistance and eventually
fleeing to Switzerland in September 1943 with the Gestapo on his
heels. Yet an undeserved reputation for having been a collaborator
would haunt him for the rest of his life, and this perception undoubtedly played a major role in preventing his work from gaining
the recognition in France that it deserved. Still, however unjust
some criticisms of Jouvenel's role in a dark period of French and
European life may be, legitimate questions persist about the ultimate adequacy of his practical judgment. The sympathetic student
of Jouvenel is torn between profound admiration for the wise and
humane political philosopher and unavoidable discomfort with the
poor practical judgment that he regularly displayed in the opening
and closing periods of his intellectual career.

In my judgment, Jouvenel's status as a political thinker stands
or falls with one's judgment of the major books and essays he produced between the mid-1940s and mid-1960s. During this period
Jouvenel wrote his enduring works of political philosophy and social science and became one of the preeminent conservative liberal
thinkers of the age. During these years, his learned and elegant
writings unfailingly displayed principled moderation and political
good sense. Jouvenel seemed to have found his mature voice and
to have overcome his youthful flirtation with antiliberal politics.
But this is not the end of the story.

After 1968, Jouvenel once again drifted to the Left. He expressed some sympathy for the student rebels of May 1968, those unremitting critics of liberal or bourgeois society. Jouvenel had no illusions whatsoever about Castro or Mao or any of the other tyrants so beloved by the radical Left at the time. But he adopted a slightly obsequious attitude toward the young (the "future masters" of society as he put it in a January 1972 interview with *L'Express*).[5] Some of this undoubtedly can be attributed to Jouvenel's larger distaste for Gaullism and the cult of personality that tended to infuse that political movement. Jouvenel did not doubt de Gaulle's commitment to democratic institutions. But he remained wary of "the monarchization of command" that characterized the political life of the French Fifth Republic.[6] Jouvenel was also a committed partisan of European integration who was allergic to nationalism in all its forms. He identified the cult of the nation with the rise of state power and the unleashing of the worst social passions. If he cured himself of youthful pacifism, he nonetheless remained suspicious of appeals to the grandeur of the nation-state. His indulgence toward "1968" also reflected his growing environmental and ecological concerns. The New Left's revolt against consumer society and the "organizational imperative" appealed to Jouvenel's sense that modern economic development had come at the price of balanced social development and authentic human happiness.

In the 1970s, the drift to the Left continued. Jouvenel even warmed to the "Common Program" of the united Left (the Socialists and Communists under the leadership of François Mitterrand), which promised nationalization of business enterprises and massive efforts at government redistribution of income. This was an immense about-face for a thinker who had been one of the charter members of Hayek's Mont Pélerin society and who had penned the most powerful moral critique of collectivism written in the postwar period, *The Ethics of Redistribution* (1952). But as we shall see, Jouvenel never really abandoned his opposition to nationalization, as his final major work makes clear enough. Something other than an intellectual conversion to socialism must account for Jouvenel's indulgence toward the Left in the 1970s and 1980s. Whatever his motives, Jouvenel insisted to anyone who would listen that he had always shared the ideals of the Left. After the victory of the Socialists and Communists in the 1981 presidential and parliamentary elections, Jouvenel trumpeted his friendship with such prominent socialist politicians as Jacques Delors.[7] This desperate desire to be perceived as a man of the Left is not fully appreciated by most of Jouvenel's admirers in the Anglo-American world, which is not surprising, given that Jouvenel's best work dates from his conservative period. Indeed, only one subsequent book, a meditation on the legacy of Marx and Engels, shows any imprint of Jouvenel's partial drift to the Left in his later years.

What is one to make of this curious shift toward positions that Jouvenel had spent his entire postwar career opposing? Why this apparently deep-seated need to curry favor with the intellectual and political Left after decades of pursuing an admirably independent line as one of France's few genuinely liberal thinkers? Paradoxically enough, when the renaissance of liberal political philosophy began to unfold in France after 1975, fuelled by the publication of Solzhenitsyn's *The Gulag Archipelago* and the belated acknowledgment of the totalitarian propensities of Marxism, Jouvenel was too busy rehabilitating himself to really notice. There is something tragic about the weakness of character that led to such political misjudgments—and desperate reinventions.

The fullest exploration of this enigma can be found in Jean-François Revel's 1997 *Mémoires,* which is subtitled *Le voleur dans la maison vide* (The Thief in the Empty House).[8] Revel was an editorial advisor at Éditions Robert Laffont when that publishing house released *Un voyageur dans le siècle* (A Voyager in the Century), Jouvenel's own memoir of his life before 1945. Revel met Jouvenel in 1976, when Jouvenel was both attempting to come to terms with his prewar career and drifting leftward. Revel, who had read and was an admirer of Jouvenel's classic works of political philosophy, was deeply disturbed by what seemed to him to be a profound weakness of political judgment on Jouvenel's part. Revel's account of Jouvenel in *Le voleur dans la maison vide* is a damning indictment of the later Jouvenel, a portrait of a weak-willed if charming and amiable man whose judgment was corrupted by both "ideology" and "pathology."[9] Revel convincingly argues that Jouvenel's shift toward the Left was related to his failure to adequately come to terms with his past. His lack of genuine introspection and a somewhat narcissistic concern with his reputation had led him to try to reinvent himself. But in the course of this rather ungenerous indictment, Revel significantly exaggerates the extent of Jouvenel's ideological transformation. He writes disdainfully about Jouvenel's *Marx et Engels,* which was published by Commentaire Julliard in 1983 in a book series edited by Jean-Claude Casanova, a disciple of Raymond Aron.[10] Revel, who had turned this book down when he was an editor at Laffont, dismissively describes it as an "elegy of

Marx" and "even indulgent about Stalin."[11] This, to say the least, is a gross mischaracterization.

Despite the tone of scrupulous respect for Marx and Engels that characterizes Jouvenel's book throughout, as well as the author's tendency to bend over backwards to be generous to the founding fathers of communism, *Marx et Engels* is decidedly non-Marxist in its core presuppositions. A careful reader will discern no fundamental break whatsoever between the principles and positions that Jouvenel enunciates in it and the spirit of his great postwar writings on political philosophy. The book is recognizably "Jouvenelian" in style, tone, and point of view. Jouvenel had not become a Marxist (or Stalinist!), as Revel rather fantastically intimates. His fluctuating judgment has much more to do with weakness of character (evident in his excessive desire to be accepted) than it has to do with any essential change of ideological orientation. Revel's critique of Jouvenel is too summary because too hurried.

In truth, *Marx et Engels* is a thoughtful and impressive if finally flawed book. It is also undoubtedly a curious one. For one thing, the timing of the book is perplexing. It might have been necessary for a non-leftist French thinker writing about Marx in the 1950s and '60s to go out of his way to express his admiration for the author of *Das Kapital* if he hoped to gain a hearing in "respectable" intellectual quarters. But by the time Jouvenel's book appeared in 1983, Marx was no longer the master thinker who lorded over French intellectual life. The thinking public was in a mood to welcome a balanced and critical engagement with Marx's manifold philosophical and political limitations. If anything, the slightly apologetic tone of Jouvenel's treatment of Marx probably contributed to the fact that at the time of its publication the book had next to no impact on French discussions of politics or political theory.

Jouvenel's book also fails to confront the deepest philosophical flaws of Marxism: it provides no systematic critique of the materialism, economism, and historicism that pervade Marx's work. This failure to go to the heart of things is all the more perplexing because Jouvenel's grounding in classical and Christian thought, so evident in his great works of political philosophy, put him in an excellent position to expose the moral and intellectual limitations of the Marxist project. It is surprising, for example, that Jouvenel never develops his earlier and quite compelling critique of "the inner contradiction" at the heart of Marxian socialism that he had explored to such great effect in *The Ethics of Redistribution*.[12] Here and there, to be sure, Jouvenel provides incisive criticisms of Marx and Engels. For example, he dissents from their arbitrary reduction of civilization to the sole desideratum of the conquest of nature and the development of the means of production; he notes that by these materialist criteria alone neither Periclean Athens nor Renaissance Florence would have qualified as civilized societies.[13] And Jouvenel repeatedly takes Marx to task for failing to appreciate that national sentiments and attachments are far more substantial and enduring influences on human history than is "proletarian consciousness."[14] He argues that one reason why Marxism has been attractive to so many in the third world is precisely because it promises a formula by which so-called underdeveloped nations can emulate the modernization that took many centuries to unfold in the liberal West. Marxism, then, is best understood as a political choice and not the product of an inexorable historical process, as its doc-trinaires had always insisted. Despite the force of these criticisms, the reader is left with the feeling that they do not go to the heart of the matter. Jouvenel's book is not radical enough.

Nonetheless, despite his affection for Marx and Engels, Jouvenel cannot finally avoid holding them partly responsible for the totali-tarian tragedies of the twentieth century. He recognizes a crucial connection between the revolutionary speculations of Marx and Engels and "the great political invention of the twentieth century," the "single party" regime.[15] At times, particularly in the chapter that explicitly addresses the question of the relationship between Marx and Stalinism (chapter 21), Jouvenel emphasizes the ways in which Communist totalitarianism entails a betrayal of the Marxist heritage.[16] He cannot believe that Marx and Engels would have favored an indefinite extension of violence and repression against the purported enemies of socialism. He rightly insists that Stalinist dogmatism and brutality would have revolted Marx. He rather less persuasively suggests that Stalin's actions were influenced more by pan-Russian nationalism than by Communist ideology (it would have been more accurate to argue that Stalin and the Bolsheviks appropriated Russian nationalism for their own ideological pur-poses, even as they continued to violently repress such traditional "Russian" institutions as the Russian Orthodox Church and an independent peasantry and intelligentsia).

Yet in the end, Jouvenel insists that there is an intimate con-nection between the denial of initiative in the intellectual realm and the denial of freedom in the economic realm. In his view, Marx failed to directly confront the political problem of the need to limit

Power and thereby undermined the "political acquisition" of the West,[17] the precious and always fragile protections against intellectual, spiritual, and political despotism. Marx, who eloquently warned (in *The Civil War in France*) against the tendency of the state to swallow civil society like a "boa constrictor," contributed to the establishment of a revolutionary order that massively reinforced the size and ambition of an unprecedented omnipotent state. In chapter 11 of *Marx et Engels*, titled "Towards Oriental Socialism," Jouvenel expresses an ambiguous and measured judgment of the responsibility of Marx for the depravities of so-called Marxist regimes: "Some will say that Marx had not wished this [the totalitarian state]; and without doubt they are right. Others will say that Marx's work leads there logically and I believe that they are not wrong." He tellingly adds that Marx's thought "opens the road to despotic regimes, involuntarily but logically."[18] Aron, Jouvenel's friend and contemporary, articulates the same ambiguous judgment about the relationship between the Marxism of Marx and the totalitarianism of twentieth-century Marxist-Leninism in his posthumously published *Le Marxisme de Marx* (2002).[19]

Jouvenel also provides a persuasive explanation for this paradox. Marx was so preoccupied with the economic question, with uprooting all forms of economic exploitation, that he forgot the crucial importance of restricting political power. He dogmatically treated political authority as a simple byproduct of economic relations and thus summarily dismissed the protections against despotism that were the glory of the West. He lived in a civilized Europe that respected basic human liberties—liberties he more or less took for granted. Jouvenel reminds his readers that Marx took refuge in

England, the home, par excellence, of political and intellectual liberty. Acquitted by a German jury in 1849 for his activities during the revolution of 1848, he would not have fared so well "before a Hitlerian or Stalinist tribunal."[20] This Samson of revolutionary subversion, as Jouvenel suggestively calls him, wished to tear down all the walls of a supposedly corrupt bourgeois order.[21] But like Samson he was blind, first and foremost to "the precious juridical and moral edifice" that constituted the premodern and modern traditions of constitutionalism.[22] The heart and soul of the West lay in the constitutionalist affirmation of the need for rights and privileges to limit the encroachments of Power. Is it any accident that the revolutionary destruction of this complex edifice, the centuries-old heritage of constitutional liberty, would give rise to something worse than even oriental despotism? Until the end of his life Jouvenel remained perplexed by Marx's utter blindness to this political problem. How could a self-described proponent of human emancipation support the total concentration of both economic and political power in the hands of the revolutionary state? How could he then reasonably expect this state to wither away? Above all, "Why . . . was Marx not disquieted by a power which was so total? It is for me an unsolvable enigma."[23]

With much less polemical intent, Jouvenel thus renews the critique of Marxism put forward by a whole series of nineteenth-century authors, including Proudhon and Bakunin. These thinkers accurately predicted that if put into practice Marx's ideas would lead to what Leszek Kolakowski has called "state slavery."[24] One does not solve the problem of monopoly by making the state the owner of everyone and everything. Jean-François Revel is simply wrong when he suggests that *Marx et Engels* is an apology for Marxism in any of its forms.

In these penetrating reflections on the blindness of Marx, the reader of *Marx et Engels* hears the distinctive voice of a true liberal and a great political thinker. Whatever the political twists and turns of his final years, Jouvenel remained a principled opponent of intellectual and political despotism.

In a revealing interview with the French journal *L'Expansion* published in January 1970, Jouvenel argued that modern thought "attaches too much importance to institutions" and not enough to the crucial place of manners in the humane ordering of society.[25] In particular, Marx was mistaken to believe that "all oppression would disappear with the abolition of private property."[26] It is disappointing, to say the least, that in his only systematic confrontation with the Marxism of Marx, Jouvenel failed to muster the courage to subject Marx's sociologism to the thoroughgoing criticism that it merits. Marx's atheism and materialism led him to confuse the abolition of private property with genuine respect for the spiritual dignity of man. The author of *On Power* and *Sovereignty* never forgot this fundamental truth, as the 1970 interview well attests. Whatever its ultimate limits, Jouvenel's last book reveals the fundamental continuity of his post-1945 writings. Beginning with *On Power*, Jouvenel's work is a sustained moral and political reflection on the problem of freedom and despotism. There is finally nothing ideological or pathological about this enterprise.

Conclusion

The Jouvenel scholar is obliged to address the question of the solidity and reliability of Jouvenel's practical judgment when faced with the soul-wrenching choices that inevitably confronted a voyager in the twentieth century. Even the most sympathetic exegete cannot deny that Jouvenel's practical engagement with the politics of his time often lacked the measure, nobility, and sure-footedness that was conveyed on nearly every page of his classic writings in political philosophy. There is an undeniable tension between the high-minded liberalism that characterizes his great works of political reflection and the intermittent indulgence to-ward political extremism that marred his choices in the period before World War II and to a lesser extent during the twilight of his life. What Daniel Halévy said about Maurice Barrès can be said with equal justice about Bertrand de Jouvenel: "He is never totally in what he has written."[27] In Jouvenel's case, it is not unjust to state that the political philosopher was significantly more illuminating, measured, and sure of himself than the political actor and partisan. In the end, there remains something enigmatic about Jouvenel's character. This kind, cultivated, and charming man doubted his own judgments and thirsted for a recognition that would finally be denied him in his native France.

One does not have to share Jean-François Revel's overwrought judgment of Bertrand de Jouvenel in order to recognize that weak-ness of character and a propensity to unsteady judgment go some way in explaining his dizzying political oscillations . But Jouvenel's wavering political commitments also reflect a healthy and prin-

cipled openness to the complexity of political life. To his credit,
Jouvenel came to reject the twin theoretical extremes of libertarianism and collectivism. As Eric Roussel has wisely observed,
Jouvenel's mature thought was informed by a dialectical movement
between support for prudent political measures to modify the anarchy of the market and shape a more humane future, on the one
hand, and steadfast opposition to the authoritarianism that accompanies political and economic collectivism, on the other.[28] In
the 1930s, Jouvenel's social conscience was galvanized by the tepid,
ineffectual response of the Western democracies to the economic
and social crisis then enveloping the world. Eager for effective action to address this crisis, Jouvenel was perhaps insufficiently sensitive to the dangers that inevitably arise when an activist state goes
too far in restricting the multiple initiatives emanating from civil
society. But the terrible experience of total war and totalitarian
tyranny taught Jouvenel the monstrousness of all efforts to "deify
Power."[29] Free peoples, he wrote in 1965, must be acutely aware "of
the dangers of an unlimited imperium. The greater one allows the
public power to be, the greater must be the safeguards against the
harm which it can do."[30]

Jouvenel's postwar political writings admirably succeeded in
combining principled opposition to collectivism with support for
prudent political measures designed to manage social change and
promote the common good. In his view, however, a liberal state
should never aim to substitute itself for the free choices and judgments of responsible individuals. Nor should it undermine the rich
array of intermediate associations and social groupings that limit
state power and channel individual initiatives in socially construc-

tive ways. The true liberal, he declares, "places his confidence" in the prudence of individuals informed by conscience and instructed by the rule of law.[31] But if he rejects collectivism in all its forms, he also recognizes that the public Authorities have a moral responsibility to provide education and "credit" (i.e., opportunities and incentives that do not undermine individual initiative) to all citizens. By doing so, they give each member of the political community "the means to use his liberty." A liberal society worthy of its name must aim to render "the right and the means of independent action to the greatest number." Such was the noble "object of liberal politics" according to Jouvenel.

In my view, Jouvenel's theoretical articulation of this dialectic of energetic and effective government on the one hand, and eternal vigilance against the encroachments of Power on the other, is beyond reproach. At the same time, Jouvenel was not satisfied with what political theorists call "negative liberty." He constantly reminded the citizens of the democracies that self-government is a moral challenge demanding the cultivation of the highest virtues. Jouvenel's political thought is difficult to classify because it remained true to the constitutionalist imperative to limit Power while recognizing that the state has a vital role to play in shaping a future hospitable to the common good and allowing a place for "the amenities of life."

Jouvenel's political reflection, therefore, was the furthest thing from doctrinaire and could accommodate a wide range of political commitments. From one perspective, his principles appear to allow for excessive flexibility and a debilitating refusal to remain true to a settled point of view. From another perspective, his refusal to simplify the complexities of social and political life allowed him to escape the tyranny of the Left-Right dichotomy and to think and breathe freely within the shifting constraints and possibilities of the democratic city. As Dennis Hale and Marc Landy have noted, Jouvenel's "voice belongs neither to the left nor to the right, and his writing has therefore the freshness and simplicity of the best teaching. . . . He shares with the left a deep concern with reducing human misery and ecological depredation, and he shares the left's belief in the need for government-directed economic planning. On the other hand, he shares the right's abiding suspicion of state power and its belief in the superiority of the market as the normal method for economic decision making. He is neither a romantic reactionary nor a celebrator of progress."[32]

Indeed, Jouvenel freely accepted the inevitability of what he called the "productivist" or progressive society, marked by myriad initiatives and sources of change. At the same time, he crafted a political science that aimed to preserve those preconditions of the good life which were imperiled by these very innovations. In Jouvenel's considered judgment, a balanced social order must have a place both for the innovator, whom he called *Dux*, and the stabilizer, whom he called *Rex* (this distinction is the subject of a particularly suggestive chapter in the first part of *Sovereignty*). Jouvenel's mature writings also teach moderation by revealing the fragility of a liberal civilization that believed itself to represent the pinnacle of modern progress. In that regard, his writings continue to speak to us, since nothing suggests that we have arrived at the end of history.

But if Jouvenel repeatedly chastized modern political thought for its "presumption,"[33] for its tendency to aim too high and to forget the limits inherent in the human condition, he no less vigorously took it to task for aiming too low, for lacking the imagination to even raise the questions of the good life, civic friendship, and the common good that were so central to the tradition of classical political philosophy. In an impressive reflection titled "On the Citizen,"[34] published posthumously in *Itinéraire*, Jouvenel takes aim at both the pride and the timidity of the modern theorist. In his view, the modern intellectual often lacks the discipline and moral imagination to "to linger over the organizable substance of reality."[35] Deformed by a unique "marriage of sloth and pride," he creates "models" of the human future that have "no relationship to society and which are only the representation of his creative mind."[36] The "idealism" of the utopian intellectual is at once "exhilarating" for the mind of the "creative" intellectual and "ruinous" for the health of society.[37] Here we see Jouvenel renewing Tocqueville's earlier critique of the abstract rationalism of "literary" intellectuals in light of the twentieth century's political tragedies.[38]

But although Jouvenel rejects utopianism, both because it allows the theorist to evade the difficult and demanding work of thinking about concrete political life and because it all too readily gives rise to monstrous social experimentation, he never equated utopianism with a salutary concern for the moral foundations of a free society. His work brings together antiutopianism and a lively attentiveness to the requirements of the common good, especially the affections that bind citizens one to another.

Jouvenel faults modern political inquiry for failing to ask the full range of truly important questions. It has been so preoccupied with the question of political legitimacy, the question of *who* has the right to rule, that it has almost completely neglected the far more fundamental matter of *how* authority ought to be exercised within a decent and free political community.[39] Because of this preoccupation with the source of power at the expense of a concern with its proper exercise, modern political theorists have next to nothing to say about civic and moral education, the primary theme of premodern political philosophy. In "On the Citizen," Jouvenel reflects on the baleful consequences of this silence about the moral dimensions of democratic politics.

The modern citizen, like the ancient one, is said to govern himself. This is a moral task of the highest order, but it is a task largely forgotten by a political science preoccupied with institutional structures and afraid to make "unscientific" "value judgments."[40] As a contributor to the "general will," as a shareholder in the public sovereignty, the citizen of modern democracy is at least in principle "master of the fate of his near and dear and of the destiny of his people."[41] But he typically lacks a sufficient awareness of the responsibilities that accompany any claim to govern. The contrast with his historical forebears could not be more striking. Following Plutarch and Rousseau, Jouvenel reminds us of just how acutely aware Roman senators were of their civic dignity, of their awesome political responsibilities. They could repeat with the ambassador of Pyrrhus that he had "found in them an assembly of kings."[42] And Jouvenel reminds us that the treatises on government under the old regime spoke incessantly about the responsibilities of monarchs to God, their subjects, and the temporal common good. Rather than emancipating the king to rule as he saw fit, the political science of the old regime taught moral restraint and heroic self-overcoming. The theorists of the old regime knew a monarch could be guilty of the worst "injustice and imprudence."[43] They thus "lavished" him with warnings about the consequences of placing his own will above the requirements of the common good.[44] "One asked of him a moral effort that elevated him above the human condition: he must act as a king, only having regard for the good of his flock, wrenching himself from the solicitations of his particular temperament, mastering his passions, forgetting his resentments, deaf to the importunities of his favorites."[45] Jouvenel appreciates that all-too-fallible human beings could not practice this "heroic discipline" without "grave failings."[46] But the specific merit of the political thought of the old regime was that it placed "the obligations of Power" squarely before the eyes of those who had a special responsibility to promote and preserve the common good.[47] For its part, modern constitutionalism had the merit of knowing that these responsibilities were, in practice, too much for any single human being to bear. But its advocates came to forget what Montesquieu and Rousseau still knew, that virtue remained a necessary *principle*, even if attenuated or qualified, of any sustainable self-governing political order. Modern men are no longer cognizant of the fact that citizenship still demands *some* self-overcoming, if not the austere patriotism of the ancient citizen or the regal self-command of the Christian monarchs of old.

In a democratic society, the public power is said to belong to all. But in practice "the princely power" is devolved unevenly to different segments of society.[48] A small group of men and women are citizens in the full Aristotelian sense of the term ("ruling and being ruled in turn"); the rest are typically "passive citizens" indifferent to the ordinary course of civic life.[49] The high-minded rhetoric of democratic legitimacy thus masks the oligarchic reality of the modern public square. But the division of the city into the few and the many is not the deepest source of our modern discontents. That can be located in the fact that no sustained effort is made to educate those "active participants in the Sovereign Power."[50] Those who are citizens in the full sense of the term, whether government ministers, journalists, or party functionaries, too often confuse their public roles with personal self-aggrandizement or the demands of ideological sectarianism. But "one cannot reproach them with being deaf to moral exhortations"[51] because modern political science no longer sees it as its mission to "alert the Great," to bring them to their civic senses.[52] Modern political science long ago abandoned any aspiration to be a "moral Science."[53] A prisoner of egalitarian dogma and democratic abstractions, the modern political scientist no longer appreciates that the education of "the Great," of those who are in a position to "move other men," is a permanent requirement of the political common good. The modern intellectual prefers to dream of utopian alternatives to prosaic liberal society while the academic social scientist is so afraid of violating the spirit of "neutrality" that guides his craft that he refuses to articulate the principles that give order to the free initiatives of men.[54] The result of this intellectual abdication is a kind of moral anarchy in which the will of men is severed from the natural objects of human choice.

Jouvenel is one of the few political philosophers of the age who truly appreciated the moral grandeur inherent in democratic political life. Democracies require citizens—and thus the continuing cultivation of moral and intellectual virtue. In every time and

place a preeminent task of political science is to restrain the imprudence and injustice of the few and the many alike. And Power can
only be truly limited if it is conscious of a "common good" before
which it is ultimately obliged to bow. Bertrand de Jouvenel has
shown us that it is possible to renew our inquiry into the political
good in a manner that respects the political achievements of modern liberal civilization. His elegant and instructive writings illustrate that the old and new political and philosophical dispensations are not forever destined to be strangers, bridged only by a
melancholy reflection on the tragic political condition of man.
Jouvenel succeeded in bringing old gods to a new city, deities that
are in the contemporary world desperately needed.

NOTES

Preface

1. Bertrand de Jouvenel, *The Pure Theory of Politics*, foreword by Daniel J. Mahoney (Indianapolis, IN: Liberty Fund, 2000), xix.
2. See the addendum to *The Pure Theory of Politics* ("The Myth of the Solution"), 275–76.
3. Bertrand de Jouvenel, *On Power: The Natural History of Its Growth* (Indianapolis, IN: Liberty Fund, 1993), 350.

Chapter 1

1. Jouvenel's "Quelles Europe voulons-nous?" originally appeared in *La Gazette de Lausanne* on May 24, 1945 and is reprinted in Bertrand de Jouvenel, *Itinéraire* (1928–1976), ed. Eric Roussel (Paris: Plon, 1993), 316–18.
2. See their introduction to *The Nature of Politics: Selected Essays of Bertrand de Jouvenel* (New Brunswick, NJ: Transaction, 1992), 1.
3. Pierre Manent, *Les libéraux*, 2nd ed. (Paris: Gallimard, 2001), 855–56.
4. Benjamin Constant, *Principles of Politics Applicable to all Governments* (1810 edition), trans. Dennis O'Keefe (Indianapolis, IN: Liberty Fund, 2003), bk. 1, chap. 6, 20.
5. The biographical account of Jouvenel in this chapter draws upon his indispensable memoir *Un voyageur dans le siècle: 1903–1945*, written with the aid of Jeannie Malige (Paris: Robert Laffont, 1979); Dennis Hale and Marc

Landy's thoughtful and comprehensive introduction to *The Nature of Politics: Selected Essays of Bertrand de Jouvenel*; Eric Roussel's anthology of Jouvenel's writings, *Itinéraire: 1928–1976*; Dominique Bourg's preface ("Bertrand de Jouvenel et l'écologie politique") to Bertrand de Jouvenel, *Arcadie: Essais sur le mieux-vivre* (Paris: Gallimard, 2002); and Pierre Hassner's remarkable entry on Bertrand de Jouvenel in the "Biographical Supplement" to the *International Encyclopedia of the Social Sciences*, vol. 18 (New York: MacMillan / Free Press, 1979), 358–62.

6. This claim about the "classical" character of Jouvenel's political science needs to be qualified. Jouvenel's work certainly highlights the existential importance of politics, but it does not emphasize the primacy of the political regime in the manner of Aristotle, Leo Strauss, or Raymond Aron (but see Jouvenel's 1963 essay "On the Evolution of Forms of Government" in *The Nature of Politics*, 166–220). Accepting the modern separation of political and social spheres as his provisional starting point, Jouvenel presents the political scientist as the "suzerain of the social field, who runs but a small part of the realm, but must oversee the whole, as any trouble arising in any other part must seep into his own" (see Jouvenel's 1965 essay "Political Science and Prevision" in *The Nature of Politics*, quotation from p. 149.). The political scientist is obliged to be a "generalist" rather than a technician or "specialist" precisely because he has a special responsibility to anticipate "trouble" and to promote a rapprochement among the various analysts of the modern social field. Jouvenel's political scientist is thus something of a reluctant suzerain. Jouvenel's political philosopher, in contrast, is far more ambitious: his theme is nothing less than the political good in all its diverse manifestations. Political science and political philosophy, so understood, are crucial for maintaining the wholeness of human vision and for sustaining a sense of the common good within increasingly individualistic modern societies.

7. I am indebted to Wilson Carey McWilliams for this observation.

8. Jouvenel, *Un voyageur dans le siècle*, 250.

9. Jouvenel would depart from the Mont Pélerin Society in 1960 precisely because he could not endorse its "libertarian" disdain for the very idea of the "public good," or what he came to perceive as its implaccable hostility to every initiative, however necessary or salutary, that was undertaken by public authorities.

10. See note 5.

11. See Hassner, "Bertrand de Jouvenel," 358.

12. Sarah Boas was a protégé of Milan Stefanik, who along with Thomas Masaryk and Edward Benes created the modern Czechoslovakian state. See *Un voyageur dans le siècle*, 47–50.

13. See Jouvenel's discussion of Colette in *Un voyageur dans le siècle*, 54–58.

14. See Hassner, "Bertrand de Jouvenel," 359.

15. Jouvenel, *Un voyageur dans le siècle,* 16.

16. Ibid., 19.

17. Jouvenel, *Un voyageur dans le siècle* was originally intended to be a two-volume autobiography, with the second volume exploring Jouvenel's life after 1945. Unfortunately, the second part of this work never saw the light of day.

18. Jouvenel, *Un voyageur dans le siècle*, 17.

19. See Jouvenel's remarkable portrait of his generation in *Un voyageur dans le siècle*, 76–85.

20. Ibid., 17.

21. Ibid., 16–17.

22. On this point, see our discussion in chapter 7.

23. Jouvenel, *Un voyageur dans le siècle*, 16.

24. Ibid., 89. *L'économie dirigée: Le programme de la nouvelle génération* appeared from the Parisian publisher Librairie Valois in 1928. In the words of Roussel, "the best pages" from this work can be found in *Itinéraire*, 77–96.

25. Jouvenel, *Itinéraire*, 91.

26. Ibid.

27. Ibid.

28. See chapter 7 for a fuller discussion of Jouvenel's lifelong preoccupation with the disastrous moral and political effects of unemployment.

29. Bertrand de Jouvenel, *La crise du capitalisme américain* (Paris: Gallimard, 1933).

30. This description of Jouvenel's turn to a mature antitotalitarianism freely draws on my introduction to *Sovereignty: An Inquiry into the Political Good* (Indianapolis, IN; Liberty Fund, 1997), which was written in conjunction with David M. DesRosiers.

31. See Jouvenel, *Un voyageur dans le siècle*, 297–303, for Jouvenel's account of his involvement in Doriot's political movement.

32. Ibid., *Un voyageur dans le siècle*, 74.

33. See Zeev Sternhell's *Neither Right Nor Left: Fascist Ideology in France* (Princeton, NJ: Princeton University Press, 1986). Sternhell's book was

originally published in French by Gallimard in 1983. His attribution of a fellow-travelling "fascist ideology" to Jouvenel led the French political philosopher to bring a libel action against the Israeli historian in 1983. Jouvenel won the suit but was awarded minimal damages, perhaps reflecting the inherent ambiguity of both the case and of a particularly anguished period in French national life. Raymond Aron, the greatest French political thinker of the age, testified on Jouvenel's behalf at the libel trial on October 17, 1983, and died of a heart attack as he descended the stairs of the Palais de justice in Paris. Jouvenel movingly comments on Aron's final act of friendship in "Une dernière image," *Commentàire*, no. 28–29, February 1985, 119–21.

34. Bertrand de Jouvenel, *Après la défaite* (Paris: Plon, 1941). In addition, see Hassner's comments on page 359 of his article on Jouvenel.

35. See Jouvenel, *Un voyageur dans le siècle*, 368, 374–75. General Navarre, the former head of the intelligence service of the French army (the SR) has confirmed the veracity of Jouvenel's account.

36. Ibid., 445.

37. *Du Pouvoir: Histoire naturelle de sa croissance* was originally published in Geneva by Edition du Cheval Ailé in February 1945. It was subsequently republished by the Parisian publisher Hachette in 1972 and has remained in print in France to this day. An English-language edition of *On Power: Its Nature and the History of Its Growth*, ably translated by J. F. Huntington, first appeared in 1948 from the Viking Press. *On Power* was later reissued by Beacon Press in 1962 and again by Liberty Fund in 1993. It is the latter, readily available edition, that will be cited throughout this text.

38. Bertrand de Jouvenel, *The Ethics of Redistribution* (Cambridge: Cambridge University Press, 1952). Liberty Fund reissued the book in 1990 with an introduction by the well-known English social theorist John Gray. As we will show in chapter 5, *The Ethics of Redistribution* is often misinterpreted as a work in the "classical liberal" tradition when in fact it highlights and criticizes the radically individualist assumptions underlying both capitalist and collectivist approaches to political economy.

39. See Bertrand de Jouvenel, *De la souveraineté: À la recherche du bien politiqu*e (Paris: M.T. Génin, 1955). J. F. Huntington's elegant translation of *Sovereignty: An Inquiry into the Political Good* was released by Cambridge University Press in the United Kingdom and by the University of Chicago Press in the United States in 1957. Liberty Fund reissued the book in 1997, and it is that edition which will be cited throughout this text.

40. *The Pure Theory of Politics* (originally published in the United States by Yale University Press in 1963) was written in English and subsequently translated into French as *De la politique pure* (Paris: Calmann-Lèvy, 1963). Throughout, I will cite the Liberty Fund edition published in 2000.

41. See Jouvenel, *On Power*, bk. 6, chap. 19, 396–418.

42. See Bertrand de Jouvenel, "Pure Politics Revisited," *Government and Opposition* 15, no. 3–4 (Summer-Autumn 1980). Jouvenel understood political science to be a "moral science," or more precisely, a "natural Science dealing with moral agents" (see *Sovereignty*, 368). But as *The Pure Theory of Politics* indicates, he also saw the need to confront the elementary phenomena of politics without a priori moral expectations or evaluations. As he put it in the 1980 essay "Pure Politics Revisited," "One must return to elementary political phenomena, in their raw state, in order to learn how to polish them." The political scientist cannot be an effective "guardian of civility" (*Pure Theory*, 276), he will be powerless to convey sober moral advice to political and social actors, unless he appreciates the myriad ways in which "men move men." He is thus obliged to come to terms with the full range of human "behavior" before he ascends to his "moral pulpit" (*Pure Theory*, 44). But Jouvenel repeatedly took mainstream social science to task for its one-sided preoccupation with "weak" political behavior, such as voting patterns and the judicial process. Behavioral political science tended to take the achievements of liberal democracy for granted and was generally averse to focusing on "strong political behavior . . . inspired by a strong passion, and to which men throw themselves wholeheartedly" (*Pure Theory*, 48). For all its claims to factual rigor, "behavioralism" too often presupposed unacknowledged assumptions about the inevitably "progressive" direction of human history.

43. See Hassner, "Bertrand de Jouvenel," 359.

44. See chapter 8 of Jouvenel, *Sovereignty*, "Of Social Friendship," particularly 147–53, as well as the fuller discussion of the "prison of the corollaries" in chapter 3 of this book.

45. Bertrand de Jouvenel, *Marx et Engels: La longue marche* (Paris: Commentaire/ Julliard, 1983). I explore the controversies surrounding Jouvenel's last major work in the final chapter of this book.

46. Jouvenel, *Sovereignty*, 236.

47. See the interview with Jouvenel ("Comment devient-on Bertrand de Jouvenel") that appeared in *L'Express* (January 17–23, 1972) and that was

republished in *Itinéraire*, 20–35. The quote is from page 22.

48. Ibid.

49. The interview ("La civilisation du XXIe siécle") appeared in *L'Expansion* in January 1970 and is reprinted in *Itinéraire*, 474–78.

50. See Bertrand de Jouvenel, *La civilisation de puissance* (Paris: Fayard, 1976) and the notebook entry of the same name in *Itinéraire*, 436–38.

51. Jouvenel, *Itinéraire*, 480.

52. Bertrand de Jouvenel, *Revoir Hélène* (Paris: Robert Laffort, 1986).

53. See the June 1970 *L'Expansion* interview in *Itinéraire*, 475–76.

54. See Jouvenel, *The Pure Theory of Politics*, xix, 21, 84–85, 99–100, 104, 107, 130, 136–37, 151, 181–83, and 186 for Jouvenel's engagement with Thucydides and Shakespeare, "the geniuses who have immortally portrayed the drama of Politics."

55. Ibid., 242–64.

56. See Jouvenel, *Sovereignty*, 238–57.

57. See Jouvenel, *Itinéraire*, 33.

58. Ibid.

59. Jouvenel, *Sovereignty*, 317.

60. See Jouvenel, *Arcadie: Essais sur le mieux-vivre* and the essays collected in Bertrand de Jouvenel, *Economics and the Good Life: Essays on Political Economy*, edited with an introduction by Dennis Hale and Marc Landy (New Brunswick, NJ: Transaction, 1999). Stephan Launay provides a particularly illuminating analysis of Jouvenel's ecological reflection in "Une génèse de la conscience écologique: La pensée de Bertrand de Jouvenel" in *Ecologie et politique,* no. 21 (Autumn-Winter 1997–1998), 101–23.

61. See the excerpt from Jouvenel's notebook titled "L'arbre" ("The Tree") in *Itinéraire*, 421–22.

52. Bertrand de Jouvenel, "La civilisation de l'éphémère" in *Itinéraire*, 422–35. The article originally appeared in *Futuribles*, no. 1–2 (Winter-Spring 1975).

63. Jouvenel, *Itinéraire*, 422–23.

64. Ibid. 430–31.

65. On this point, see Jouvenel's important September 28, 1944, article on "Collectivisme" republished in *Itinéraire*, 367–70.

66. The phrase is Aleksandr Solzhenitsyn's.

67. See Jouvenel's remarkable 1960 essay "Efficiency and Amenity" in *Economics and the Good Life*, 37–52.

68. Jouvenel, "Political Science and Prevision," in *The Nature of Politics*, 145–65.

69. Ibid., 146–47.

70. Ibid., 146.

71. Jouvenel, *Itinéraire*, 476.

72. Bertrand de Jouvenel, *L'art de conjecture* (Monaco: Editions du Rocher, 1964), published in English as *The Art of Conjecture,* trans. Nikita Lary (New York: Basic Books, 1967).

73. Jouvenel, *The Art of Conjecture*, 18.

74. Ibid., 278.

75. Ibid., 74–78 and 110–12.

76. Ibid., 134–41.

77. "The more . . . conduct is governed by custom and conforms to routine, the easier it is to foresee." Ibid., 9.

78. Ibid., 278, 293.

79. See chapters 8 and 9 of *The Art of Conjecture*, 59–82.

80. See Daniel J. Mahoney, *The Liberal Political Science of Raymond Aron* (Lanham, MD: Rowman & Littlefield, 1992) and Raymond Aron, *The Dawn of Universal History: Selected Essays from a Witness to the Twentieth Century*, trans. Barbara Bray, with an introduction by Tony Judt (New York: Basic Books, 2002).

81. The quote is from page 12 of the October 19, 1983, edition of *Le Monde*. It is cited in Hale and Landy's introduction to *The Nature of Politics*, 33.

Chapter 2

1. Montesquieu, *The Spirit of Laws*, bk. 3, chap. 9. I have cited Melvin Richter's translation in *Montesquieu: Selected Political Writings*, ed. Melvin Richter (Indianapolis, IN: Hackett Publishing Company, 1990), 132.

2. Ibid., bk. 2, chap. 4, 123.

3. Chapter 17 of *On Power* provides a particularly incisive historical analysis of the aristocratic source of liberty and its ultimate incompatibility with every form of Caesarism. See pages 352–74 of that volume.

4. Ibid., 353–54, 360–61.

5. See the translator's note to *On Power*.

6. For a representative example see the critique of *On Power* proferred by Roy Pierce in *Contemporary French Political Thought* (Oxford: Oxford University Press, 1966), 187–92.

7. Jouvenel speaks of "contre-pouvoirs" (counter-powers) that are capable of limiting and checking the usurpations of the state. See p. 464 of Jouvenel, *Du pouvoir*. Jouvenel's translator J. F. Huntington rendered this idea in English by the perfectly serviceable term "makeweight."

8. Montesquieu, *The Spirit of the Laws*, bk. 2, chap. 2.

9. See Jouvenel, *On Power*, 187. In *The Civil War in France* Marx evoked the image of the "boa constrictor" with great effect to describe the endless distension of the postrevolutionary French state.

10. See the concluding section of chapter 7 of Jouvenel, *On Power* ("The Expansionist Character of Power"), "Thought and Power: The Philosopher and the Tyrant," 145–49.

11. Hale and Landy, introduction to *The Nature of Politics*, 10.

12. See chapter 8 of Jouvenel, *On Power* ("Of Political Rivalry"), 150–167, which first appeared in January 1943 in the journal *Suisse Contemporaine*.

13. See note 6.

14. On Tocqueville's efforts to make a whole of human experience and the human soul, see Pierre Manent, "Tocqueville: Philosophe politique" in *Commentaire*, no. 107 (Autumn 2004), 586–87.

15. Hassner, "Bertrand de Jouvenel," 361.

16. See the final chapter of *On Power* ("Order and Social Protectorate") for Jouvenel's analysis of the prospects for "democratic despotism" in modern times.

17. Pierre Manent, *Cours familier de philosophie politique* (Paris: Fayard, 2001), 262. In his excellent chapter titled "Le question du communisme," Manent explores the complex set of affinities and oppositions that bind modern democracy and totalitarianism.

18. Jouvenel explores the theme of "totalitarian democracy" in chapter 14 (282–309) of *On Power*. His use of that phrase predates its subsequent popularization by J. L. Talmon by a full decade or more.

19. Stephen Launay, "Un précurseur de la critique du totalitarisme: Bertrand de Jouvenel," *Les cahiers d'histoire sociale*, no. 10 (Spring 1998), 75–86.

20. Ibid., 85.

21. Raymond Aron, *Essai sur les libertés* (Paris: Pluriel Hachette: 1977), 134.

22. Aron, *Les guerres en chaînes* (Paris: Gallimard, 1951).

23. The historian Élie Halévy brilliantly analyzed the "organization of enthusiasm" in his classic work *L'ère des tyrannies* (Paris: Gallimard, 1938) published on the eve of the Second World War.

24. On the depoliticization of contemporary Europe see Manent's magisterial *Cours familier de philosophie politique* as well as my essay "Humanitarian Democracy and the Post-Political Temptation," *Orbis* (Fall 2004), 609–24.

25. In chapters 3 and 5 I discuss Jouvenel's critically sympathetic engagement with the thought of Rousseau.

26. Rousseau, *The Discourses and Other Early Political Writings*, ed. Victor Gourevitch (Cambridge: Cambridge University Press, 1997), 19.

27. See Jouvenel, *The Nature of Politics,* for English versions of these three formidable essays.

28. "The Principate" was originally published in *Political Quarterly* 36, no. 1 (January–March 1965) and in Jouvenel's collection of essays *Du principat et autres réflexions politiques* (Paris: Hachette, 1972). I will cite the version in Jouvenel, *The Nature of Politics*, 221–54.

29. Jouvenel, *The Nature of Politics*, 233.

30. Ibid., 241–43.

31. Ibid., 241.

32. Ibid., 242.

33. Ibid., 243.

34. On the teleocratic character of modern politics, see Jouvenel, *The Nature of Politics*, 194.

35. Jouvenel, *The Nature of Politics*, 247.

36. Ibid., 240.

37. Jouvenel, *Sovereignty*, 48–66.

38. Ibid., 48–49.

39. Jouvenel, *The Nature of Politics*, 253.

40. Ibid., 254.

41. Ibid., 232–34.

Chapter 3

1. Raymond Aron, "The Liberal Definition of Liberty: Concerning F. A. Hayek's *Constitution of Liberty*" in *In Defense of Political Reason: Essays by Raymond Aron*, ed. Daniel J. Mahoney (Lanham, MD: Rowman & Littlefield, 1994).

2. Ibid., 86.

3. There are important exceptions. Religious, conservative-minded communitarians such as Jean Bethke Elshtain and Mary Ann Glendon are

penetrating critics of rights-based jurisprudence and forceful defenders of traditional moral communities.

4. More than any other recent thinker, the German émigré political philosopher Hannah Arendt is responsible for contemporary nostalgia for the classical polis as the home of authentic republicanism. Arendt valued political participation in "the public space" as the hallmark of genuine republican liberty. See her discussion of the "lost treasure" of the revolutionary tradition in chapter 6 of *On Revolution* (New York: Viking Press, 1965), 217–86.

5. See Leo Strauss, *Natural Right and History* (Chicago: University of Chicago Press, 1953) and the writings of a host of his students, including Allan Bloom, Thomas Pangle, and Stanley Rosen.

6. See Constant, "The Liberty of the Ancients Compared with that of the Moderns" in *Benjamin Constant: Political Writings*, trans. and ed. Biancamaria Fontana (Cambridge: Cambridge University Press, 1988), 307–28.

7. See Ibid., 323. Constant writes: "Individual liberty, I repeat, is the true modern liberty. Political liberty is its guarantee, consequently political liberty is indispensable. But to ask the peoples of our day to sacrifice, like those of the past, the whole of their individual liberty to political liberty, is the surest means of detaching them from the former, and, once this result has been achieved, it would be only too easy to deprive them of the latter."

8. For Constant's view of political liberty as a necessary corrective to the individualism of modern societies, see ibid., 326–28.

9. The locus classicus of contemporary "theories of justice" is of course the famous book of that name by John Rawls. Jouvenel's work shows the possibility of a very different type of liberalism, one more attuned to the affections that bind a living political order.

10. Jouvenel warns against "solutions" in politics and reminds us that prudence aims at more or less provisional "settlements." See the addendum to *The Pure Theory of Politics* titled "The Myth of the Solution," 265–76 in the Liberty Fund edition. Jouvenel's writings on political economy provide fruitful suggestions on how the good life might be cultivated within the context of "the affluent society." They illustrate in an extremely concrete way how the common good might be freed from "the prison of the corollaries." See Jouvenel, *Economics and the Good Life* and my discussion in chapter 5 of this book.

11. See the discussion of the "dimensional law of political forms" in Jouvenel, "On the Evolution of Forms of Government," in *The Nature of Politics*, 197–200.

12. See Jouvenel's discussion of Popper's *The Open Society and Its Enemies* in *Sovereignty*, 153n.

13. Jouvenel fails to appreciate sufficiently that Plato is first and foremost a partisan of the theoretical life and only subordinately and instrumentally an advocate of any particular political community. The always nuanced reader of Rousseau is a bit more heavy-handed in his reading of Plato.

14. See Jouvenel's critique of the "modern idea" of absolute sovereignty in part 3 of *Sovereignty*, 201–57.

15. See note 10.

16. See in particular Jouvenel's groundbreaking "Essai sur la politique de Rousseau" (1947), which originally appeared as an introduction to an edition of Rousseau's *Du contrat social* (Geneva: Editions du Cheval Ailé, 1947). In 1978 this text was republished as an introduction to an edition of *Du contrat social* released by the Parisian publisher Hachette. The Hachette edition also contains two other texts by Jouvenel on Rousseau. Jouvenel stands apart from most other conservative-minded readers of Rousseau in his appreciation of Rousseau as a classical moralist as well as in his refusal to identify the idea of the general will with modern totalitarianism. Jouvenel carefully distinguished Rousseau's thought from its incendiary cooptation or vulgarization by the French revolutionaries, among others.

17. Aleksandr Solzhenitsyn articulates a very similar position in his Liechtenstein address of September 14, 1993. The speech appears as an appendix to Solzhenitsyn's *"The Russian Question" at the End of the Twentieth Century* (New York: Farrar, Straus, & Giroux, 1995), 112–28.

18. On this capital point see Pierre Manent, "Totalitarianism and the Problem of Political Representation" in Manent, *Modern Liberty and Its Discontents*, trans. and ed. Daniel J. Mahoney and Paul Seaton (Lanham, MD: Rowman & Littlefield, 1998), 119–33.

19. Jouvenel fully agrees with Leo Strauss and Michael Oakeshott that Hobbes was an architect of individualist liberalism and not the father of totalitarianism in any form. See *Sovereignty*, 289–90.

20. Edmund Burke, *Reflections on the Revolution in France* (Oxford: Oxford University Press / World Classics, 1993), 96.

21. For a penetrating analysis of the modern effort to create a "neutral and agnostic" state in which power and opinion are vigorously separated, see Pierre Manent, "Préface: Situation du libéralisme" in *Les libéraux* (Paris: Gallimard / Tel, 2001), 11–16.

Chapter 4

1. Pierre Manent has remarked that liberal democracy "strik[es] a changing deal between individual and collective affirmation." See his foreword to Aurel Kolnai, *Privilege and Liberty and Other Essays in Political Philosophy*, ed. and with an introduction by Daniel J. Mahoney (Lanham, MD: Lexington Books, 1999), viii. On the salutary role of the separation of powers in "neutralizing" the absolutism of modern sovereignty, see chapter 5 ("Montesquieu and the Separation of Powers") of Manent's *An Intellectual History of Liberalism* (Princeton, NJ: Princeton University Press, 1994), 53–64.

2. On this point, see Raymond Aron's remarkable 1944 essay "The Future of Secular Religions" in Aron, *The Dawn of Universal History*, 177–201.

3. Alexis de Tocqueville, *Democracy in America*, trans. and ed. by Harvey C. Mansfield and Delba Winthrop (Chicago: University of Chicago Press, 2000), 43. Tocqueville's most eloquent discussion of the mutual compatibility of "the spirit of religion and the spirit of freedom" can be found in volume 1, part 1, chapter 2 of *Democracy in America*.

4. See Kolnai, *Privilege and Liberty and Other Essays in Political Philosophy*, 38.

5. See the author's introduction as well as the beginning of chapter 29 of Hobbes's *Leviathan*.

6. See chapter 5 ("The Triumph of the Will") of Manent's *The City of Man,* trans. Marc A. LePain (Princeton, NJ: Princeton University Press, 1998), 156–82.

7. Manent's *An Intellectual History of Liberalism* (especially 3–9) provides a particularly illuminating account of the seemingly intractable "theological-political problem" that occasioned the rise of modern liberalism.

8. For an English version of this text, see Manent, "Christianity and Democracy: Some Remarks on the Political History of Religion, or, on the Religious History of Modern Politics," in *Modern Liberty and Its Discontents*, 97–115.

9. Leo Strauss, "Progress or Return?" in Strauss, *The Rebirth of Classical Political Rationalism*, selected and introduced by Thomas L. Pangle (Chicago: University of Chicago Press), 239.

10. This striking formulation is that of the great Thomistic philosopher and theologian Jacques Maritain. See *The Peasant of the Garonne: An Old Layman Questions Himself About the Present Time* (New York: Holt, Rinehart, Winston, 1968).

11. Manent, "Christianity and Democracy," 99.

12. Ibid.

13. Michael Novak, *On Two Wings: Humble Faith and Common Sense at the American Founding* (San Francisco: Encounter Books, 2002).

14. As Tocqueville writes in volume 1, part 1, chapter 4 of *Democracy in America*, "When one wants to speak of the political laws of the United States, it is always with the dogma of the sovereignty of the people that one must begin. . . . The people reign over the American political world as does God over the universe." These passages can be found on pages 53 and 55 of the Mansfield edition.

15. Tocqueville, *Democracy in America*, vol. 1, pt. 2, chap. 10, 381.

16. Manent, "Christianity and Democracy," 100.

17. Ibid., 99.

18. Ibid.

19. Ibid., 100.

20. Ibid., 101.

21. Ibid.

22. Ibid.

23. See part 1 of Alain Besançon's *Trois tentations dans l'église* (Paris:Calmann-Lèvy, 1996) for a particularly thoughtful account of the common ground shared by Christians and liberals in the face of the totalitarian assault on reality. Despite the considerable merits of his argument, Besançon finally goes too far in conflating a historically contingent "bourgeois" civilization with the permanent requirements of human nature and the common good.

24. In their great wartime speeches, Churchill and de Gaulle went out of their way to emphasize the links between modern democracy and the moral heritage of the Christian West. They defended the dignity of man on explicitly Christian and liberal grounds. See, for example, the peroration of Churchill's "Finest Hour" speech of June 18, 1940, and de Gaulle's speech on the "crisis of civilization" delivered to the "Cercle français" at Oxford on November 25, 1941.

25. Constant as quoted in "Christianity and Democracy," 102. For the original, see Benjamin Constant, "Principles of Politics Applicable to All Representative Governments," in *Political Writings*, 176.

26. Manent, "Christianity and Democracy," 104.

27. Ibid.

28. On this widely shared sentiment of an irreversible movement from an old to a new order of things, see Manent, *An Intellectual History of Liberalism*, 8 and *The City of Man*, 51–52.

29. Hans Morgenthau, *Politics in the Twentieth Century*, vol. 3: *The Restoration of Politics* (Chicago: University of Chicago Press, 1962), 44–57. Morgenthau takes Jouvenel to task for advocating a "backward-looking romantic aristocratism which follows in the footpaths of Bonald, De Maistre, De Tocqueville, and Taine and shares in their brilliance and insights as well as in their aberrations." Morgenthau's blunt indictment ignores Jouvenel's rejection of communitarian nostalgia in all its forms.

30. Manent, *An Intellectual History of Liberalism*, 3–9.

31. Ran Halévi has captured the old regime's preoccupation with "moderation" as well as the erosion of that concern in the final decades leading up to the French Revolution. He shows that, by giving "moderation" a decidedly institutional and mechanistic cast, Montesquieu transformed and largely subverted its traditional meaning. See Ran Halévi, "La modération à l'épreuve de l'absolutisme. De l'ancien régime à la Révolution française," *Débat*, no. 109 (March-April 2000), 73–98.

32. See François Guizot, *The History of the Origins of Representative Government in Europe* (Indianapolis, IN: Liberty Fund, 2002), 292. Guizot (1787–1874) was equally a statesman, historian, and political philosopher. He was a liberal who affirmed the dignity of the political vocation and a Protestant moralist who rejected the identification of freedom with the indiscriminate right to do as one pleases. He was arguably the most preeminent liberal to affirm the necessary consonance between truth, moral responsibility, and political liberty.

33. Both essays can be found in Jouvenel, *The Nature of Politics*.

Chapter 5

1. Bernard Cazes, "L'ethique de la redistribution selon Jouvenel" in *Commentaire*, no. 52 (Winter 1990–1991), 827.

2. Joseph Cropsey, *Polity and Economy: With Further Thoughts on the Principles of Adam Smith* (South Bend, IN: St. Augustine's Press, 2001), xii.

3. On the theme of the "chrematistic society" see Jouvenel's 1961 essay, "A Better Life in the Affluent Society," which is reprinted in Jouvenel, *Economics and the Good Life*, 98–99.

4. The quote is taken from page 5 of Hale and Landy's perceptive and eloquent introduction to *Economics and the Good Life*.

5. In 1960, Jouvenel wrote to Milton Friedman to express his misgivings about an organization that held that the "state can do no good and private enterprise can do no wrong."

6. *Capitalism and the Historians* was originally published by the University of Chicago Press in 1954. Jouvenel's contribution, "The Treatment of Capitalism by Continental Intellectuals," is included in *Economics and the Good Life*, 137–54.

7. See Milton Friedman and Rose Friedman, *Two Lucky People: Memoirs* (Chicago: University of Chicago Press, 1998).

8. See chapter 14 ("The Political Philosophy of Hobbes") of Jouvenel, *Sovereignty*, esp. 290–91.

9. Jouvenel, *Economics and the Good Life*, 35.

10. Ibid., 35.

11. Ibid., 219.

12. Ibid., 218.

13. See Alexis de Tocqueville, vol. 2, pt. 4, chap. 6 of *Democracy in America*, 663.

14. Both essays have been republished in Jouvenel, *Economics and the Good Life*.

15. Jouvenel, *Arcadie*.

16. See Jouvenel, "Efficiency and Amenity," in *Economics and the Good Life*, 38 and 39.

17. Ibid., 39.

18. Ibid.

19. See "A Better Life in an Affluent Society," in *Economics and the Good Life*, 107.

20. Ibid., 110.

21. Ibid., 108.

22. Ibid., 105.

23. Jouvenel, "Efficiency and Amenity," 39.

24. Jouvenel, "The Treatment of Capitalism by Continental Intellectuals," in *Economics and the Good Life*, 139.

25. Jouvenel, *Economics and the Good Life*, 39.

26. See the balanced and informative discussion in Dominique Bourg's preface ("Bertrand de Jouvenel et l'écologie politique") to *Arcadie*, xviii.

27. The maintenance and sustenance of an "order of well-being" is the central concern of the essays that Jouvenel collected in *Arcadie*.

28. Jouvenel, *Economics and the Good Life*, 46.

29. Ibid., 116.

30. Manent, *The City of Man*, 46–49.
31. See Jouvenel's eloquent discussion of the nature of man in the concluding paragraphs of "A Better Life in an Affluent Society," in *Economics and the Good Life*, 116 and 117. The quotation is drawn from page 116.
32. Ibid., 117.
33. Jouvenel, *Economics and the Good Life*, 2.
34. Wilson Carey McWilliams, foreword to *The Nature of Politics*, 38.

Chapter 6

1. Jouvenel's starting point for "the pure theory of politics," the capacity of "men to move men," is sociological in that it does not initially distinguish between political and social phenomena. But Jouvenel's political science as a whole, of which "pure theory" is an element, never loses sight of the specificity or essentially normative character of political life.
2. Jouvenel contrasts his definition with the one put forward by Publius in *Federalist* 10. See Jouvenel, *The Pure Theory of Politics*, 236 n. 9.
3. Quoted in Jouvenel, *The Pure Theory of Politics*, 237.
4. Jouvenel, "The Principate," in *The Nature of Politics*, 234.
5. Ibid.
6. Burke, *Reflections on the Revolution in France*, 77.
7. Ibid., 76.
8. Ibid., 77.
9. Ibid.
10. Ibid., 78.
11. Ibid., 75.
12. In that work, Sartre famously celebrates "*fraternité-terreur*" as a means of overcoming the atomizing individualism of bourgeois society.
13. Georges Sorel, *Reflections on Violence,* ed. Jeremy Jennings (Cambridge: Cambridge University Press, 1999), 286.
14. Jouvenel, "On the Evolution of Forms of Government," in *The Nature of Politics*, 166–220.
15. Ibid., 170.
16. Ibid.
17. Quoted in Jouvenel, *The Nature of Politics*, 173.
18. Elie Halévy, *L'Ère des Tyrannies* (Paris: Gallimard, 1938). The title essay was originally delivered at a meeting of the French Society of Philosophy on November 28, 1936.

19. Jouvenel, "On the Evolution of Forms of Government," in *The Nature of Politics*, 175.

20. Ibid.

21. Ibid.

22. See Leszek Kolakowski, "Marxist Roots of Stalinism," in *Stalinism: Essays in Historical Interpretation,* ed. Robert C. Tucker (New Brunswick, NJ: Transaction, 1999), 283–98.

23. Aleksandr Solzhenitsyn, *The Gulag Archipelago*, vol. 1, trans. Thomas P. Whitney (New York: Harper & Row, 1974), 173–74.

24. On the shift in modern politics from the nomocratic rule of law to the teleocratic pursuit of social purposes, see Jouvenel, *The Nature of Politics*, 194.

25. See "The Spirit of Conquest and Usurpation," in *Constant: Political Writings*, esp. 26–28. Jouvenel emphasizes that, whatever their other differences, Constant, Comte, and Marx shared an essentially bourgeois understanding of the motives underlying political violence.

26. Aleksandr Solzhenitsyn, "Address to the International Academy of Philosophy, Liechtenstein, 14 September 1993," in *The Russian Question at the End of the Twentieth Century*, 128.

Chapter 7

1. The biographical account of Jouvenel in this chapter draws on his autobiography, *Un voyageur dans le siècle*; Hale and Landy's introduction to *The Nature of Politics*; and Jouvenel, *Itinéraire: 1928–1976*.

2. See the revealing interview with Jouvenel that originally appeared in *L'Express* (January 17–23, 1972) and was republished in *Itinéraire*, 20–35. The quote is from page 27.

3. See the comments of Roussel on page 77 of *Itinéraire*.

4. The phrase comes from Hale and Landy's introduction to *The Nature of Politics*, 4.

5. See *Itinéraire*, 22.

6. See Jouvenel's 1972 introduction to *Du pouvoir*, 6.

7. Several of Jouvenel's friends and colleagues have told me that they were quite surprised by Jouvenel's insistent efforts in the last years of his life to identify himself as a man of the Left.

8. Jean-François Revel, *Mémoires: Le voleur dans la maison vide* (Paris: Plon, 1997), esp. 481–86.

9. Ibid., 482.

10. Jouvenel, *Marx et Engels*. The book was completed at least by the time Jouvenel met Revel in August 1976.

11. Revel, 486.

12. Jouvenel, *The Ethics of Redistribution*, 14–17.

13. Jouvenel, *Marx et Engels*, 204. In chapter 19 of *Marx et Engels,* Jouvenel takes Marx to task for his dogmatic and philistine identification of "civilization" with "industrialization."

14. Ibid., 209–11.

15. Ibid., 218.

16. Ibid., 218–22.

17. Ibid., 146–47.

18. Ibid., 144–45.

19. See Raymond Aron's *Le Marxisme de Marx* (Paris: Éditions de Fallois, 2002), with a preface and notes by Jean-Claude Casanova and Christian Bachelier. For a detailed analysis of this work, see my "Aron, Marx, and Marxism: An Interpretation," *European Journal of Political Theory*, no. 3 (2003): 415–28.

20. Jouvenel, *Marx et Engels*, 146.

21. Ibid., 145.

22. Ibid., 147.

23. Ibid., 118.

24. On the prophetic character of the nineteenth-century anarchist critique of Marxism, see Leszek Kolakowski, "What Is Left of Socialism?" in *First Things,* October 2002, 42–46.

25. See Jouvenel's January 1970 interview with *L'Expansion*, "La civilisation du XXIe siècle," *Itinéraire*, 480.

26. Ibid.

27. I am indebted to Roussel for this citation and for discerning its relevance to Jouvenel, the man and thinker. See Jouvenel, *Itinéraire*, 41.

28. See Roussel's preface to *Itinéraire*, 13–14, as well as Jouvenel's 1972 introduction to *Du pouvoir*, 5–7.

29. See the conclusion of Jouvenel's 1965 essay "The Means of Contestation," in *The Nature of Politics*, 286.

30. Ibid.

31. In this paragraph all quotations are drawn from Jouvenel's essay, "Le liberal fait confiance à l'individu," in *Itinéraire*, 42–44. This previously unpublished essay was written in 1945 and is perfectly congruent with the argument and spirit of *Du pouvoir*.

32. See page 43 of Hale and Landy's introduction to *The Nature of Politics*.

33. See the conclusion of "Du citoyen" in Jouvenel, *Itinéraire*, 451–54.

34. This reflection on the moral foundations of democratic citizenship was left undated by Jouvenel. But its argument, style, and tone suggest that it almost certainly was written during the period when he composed *Sovereignty*, his great inquiry into the political good.

35. Ibid., 454.

36. Ibid.

37. Ibid.

38. The classic Tocquevillian critique of "literary politics" can be found in the first chapter of book 3 of *The Old Regime and the Revolution* ("How Around the Middle of the Eighteenth Century Men of Letters Became the Country's Leading Politicians and the Effects Which Resulted From This").

39. For a particularly illuminating discussion of the consequences of a one-sided emphasis on the *who* of politics at the expense of the *how,* see Jouvenel's introduction to *Sovereignty*, 1–13.

40. See the penultimate paragraph of "Du citoyen," in Jouvenel, *Itinéraire*, 453–54.

41. Ibid.

42. Ibid., 453. Compare Jouvenel's discussion with Rousseau's account of the Ambassador of Pyrrhus's remarks about the Roman senate in his famous First Discourse (*Discourse on the Sciences and Arts*) in Rousseau, *The Discourses and Other Early Political Writings*, 13–14.

43. Ibid., 452.

44. Ibid.

45. Ibid.

46. Ibid.

47. Ibid.

48. Ibid., 453.

49. Ibid.

50. Ibid.

51. Ibid.

52. Ibid.

53. For Jouvenel's description of political science as a "moral science," see Jouvenel, *Sovereignty*, 368.

54. See "Du citoyen," in Jouvenel, *Itinéraire*, 454.

INDEX

and, 59–61, 67; trust and, 60, 63, 66; tyranny and, 58. *See also* good

communism, 69; collapse of, 159; sovereignty and, 83–84; totalitarianism and, 9; tyranny and, 154–55; war, 154

communitarianism: liberalism vs., 53–54; Marxism and, 54

Comte, August, 22, 71; despotism and, 160; French Revolution and, 159; sovereignty and, 96

conjecture, art of, 21–23, 113

Constant, Benjamin, 2, 33; French Revolution and, 142, 145, 147–48, 159; liberty and, 56–57, 64; manners of politics and, 146; power and, 42; revolutionary despotism and, 4; sovereignty and, 48, 94, 105, 109

constitutionalism: checks and balances and, 85; Christian, 85; defense of, 14; liberal, 10; new, 47–51; power and, 47–51; rejuvenating, 116; separation of powers and, 108–9; sovereignty and, 104, 108–9

crise du capitalism américain, La (Jouvenel), 9

Critique of Dialectical Reason (Sartre), 150

Cropsey, Joseph, 114

Czechoslovakia, 6, 10, 153, 162–63

D

Das Kapital (Marx and Engels), 120, 167

de Gaulle, Charles, ix, 94, 164

Delors, Jacques, 165

democracy: barbarism and, 40; centralization and, 34–35; despotism and, 39; determined minority in, 13, 139; ideology and, 47; liberty and, 26; modernity and, 44; power and, 32, 34–35, 39–41, 41–44; sovereignty and, 83; totalitarianism and, 24, 44

Democracy in America (Tocqueville), 128

dependence, human, 74–77

Descartes, René, 19, 86, 104

despotism: democracy and, 39; good and, 59; power and, 46, 114; revolution and, 4, 10; sovereignty and, 25, 46; totalitarianism and, 45; West and, 26, 43

dignity: human dependence and, 74; of human nature, 81; individual, 5; liberty and, 14, 18

"dimensional law," 61–62

Directed Economy, The (*L'economie dirigée*) (Jouvenel), 8–9

"Discourse on the Arts and

ABOUT THE AUTHOR

Daniel J. Mahoney is Professor of Politics at Assumption College in Worcester, Massachusetts. A renowned expert on French political philosophy, his books include: *The Liberal Political Science of Raymond Aron: A Critical Introduction*; *De Gaulle: Statesmanship, Grandeur, and Modern Democracy*; and the critically acclaimed *Aleksandr Solzhenitsyn: The Ascent from Ideology*.